The Women Who
Fly

Aisha Lumumba

Aisha Lumumba   Atlanta, Georgia

Cover Quilt: High Cotton

Cover Design by Greenlight Design Studios

Cover Photo by Jabari Lumumba

ISBN: 0991130545
ISBN 13: 9780991130542

DEDICATION

To all the women, who have sprouted wings
in a tough situation and made it through
despite the odds.

CONTENTS

ACKNOWLEDGMENTS

I want to thank the important great artists in my life that have influenced my work so much so that I have copied their techniques in one or two of the art pieces that make up this exhibit. I pray that I forget no one as I tell you all about them.

-**Marquetta Johnson**. Marquetta has given me such a warm friendship and sister-love that is always encouraging. I used her lovely hand dyed fabric in **Wait A Minute and Winter Walk**. She also taught me some hand painting techniques that I used in **High Cotton**. **Pat's Prayer** was a project completed from one of Ms. Marquetta's teaching workshops. **Quilters Can Fly** quilt is totally inspired by the joy, tenacity and spunk she gives from her wheelchair.

-**Jan Hollins-Sullivan**. Jan has shown some ingenious use of "other fabrics." She proves that a quilt artist must use all types of fabrics. I used the layering effect of sheer fabrics that I learned from her in **High Cotton**.

-**Joyce Daniels**. Joyce made a lovely basket on one of her quilts. I was intrigued to try her technique. I used what I learned from Joyce on the basket in **High Cotton**. I am forever thankful for her ability to come up with new ways to do things and how she shares them.

-**Tony Williams**. I thank Tony for his patience as he taught me to make the feathers that I used on **Pat's Prayer**. They are not as good as his but I am still learning.

-**Marla Jackson**. Marla is a great inspiration. Her eye for creating a quilt that teaches and tells a story is extraordinary. I have tried to follow her lead.

-**Torreah Cookie Washington**. Cookie has been instrumental in helping me learn what it means to be a professional artist. She has given quilters a venue in which we can soar.

-**Dawn Williams Boyd.** Dawn has proven to be an artist that makes a very loud political statement in all of her work. I followed in her footsteps with **Cry Me A River**. The ladies of **High Cotton** and **1921** also decided to make a political statement as well. I thank Dawn for that inspiration.

The Doll makers: **Cassandra Harrison, Gloria Grandy, Angela Ferguson, Lenora Brown, Peche Brown, Deborah Grayson, Torreah Cookie Washington and Valerie Cookie Keeling Patterson** have shared the magic of doll making with me knowingly and unknowingly. I totally respect their artistic gifts and what they bring to the craft.

I am overwhelmed with joy and love for the great editors in my life. I know each of them for their love of a great read. They are even greater proof readers. Special thanks to Clara Ponder Wright, Deborah Johnson, Joyce Daniels, and Gwendolyn Payton for keen eyes and sharp thinking.

Last but not least, I always have to thank my family for the love, support, encouragement, photography, editing, marketing, layout and design, as well as patience. I cannot thank my husband, Chinyelu, enough for his quiet tolerance while I spent days creating quilts and spent night after night typing away on this book.

INTRODUCTION

Making the quilts in this series was quite an experience. I'd say one for the record book. My doll making friends say that the dolls take on their own personality. The dolls come to life and talk to them as they are making them. The dolls decide what they want to wear and/or the statement they want to make. I have experienced a little of that with my quilts in the past because one color will stand out more than others and need another color to balance it or the quilt will start out one size and then need a border that changes everything. Listening to the color or pattern demands in a quilt is one thing but to have the personality step off the quilt to tell you her story is something totally different.

It all started with the making of Party in the Park. I was excited about creating the dress. The idea of that dress was something I had been thinking about for a couple of years. I cut the pieces and started sewing them one by one. It took on a life of its own when I put the pieces together. I tried to ignore the story that was forming in my head but when I put the dress on the background she stepped off the quilt and started to talk to me. She was talking to me all the time. I thought of her when I was sleeping, when I was cooking, and even when I was doing nothing.

Shortly after hearing her story, I realized that they all would talk to me the same way. I thought I knew why I was making each one but they had more to say about that. I merely had an idea but they had a story. They all had a full story that they wanted to share. Some of the stories did not even come to me until I started to work on that particular quilt. These quilts have taken me into subjects where I usually steer clear. Some of them had a political or personal statement they wanted to make. I realized that there was no way to tell the story of struggle, pain and triumph of African women in America without touching on the effects of the political arena, social disenfranchisement, economic disparity as well as the effects that slavery has had on us. I am so grateful that I could bring them to life in this quilt series.

This series is called Only Women Have Wings. Ladies double down in hard times and awaken their inner power. Awakening that inner power makes women sprout wings. Wings are a symbol of the inner strength that comes forth in tough times. The wings are usually invisible but this exhibit gives you a rare glimpse at them. Women have been known to show extraordinary strength like lifting cars off their children or simply keeping the lights on with a waitress salary.

I am so honored that these women told me their stories so that I can share them with you. I hope you find yourself or someone you know in their voices.

This is a work of fiction. Names, characters, businesses, places, events and incidents are either the products of the author's imagination or used in a fictitious manner. Any resemblance to actual persons, living or dead, or actual events is purely coincidental.

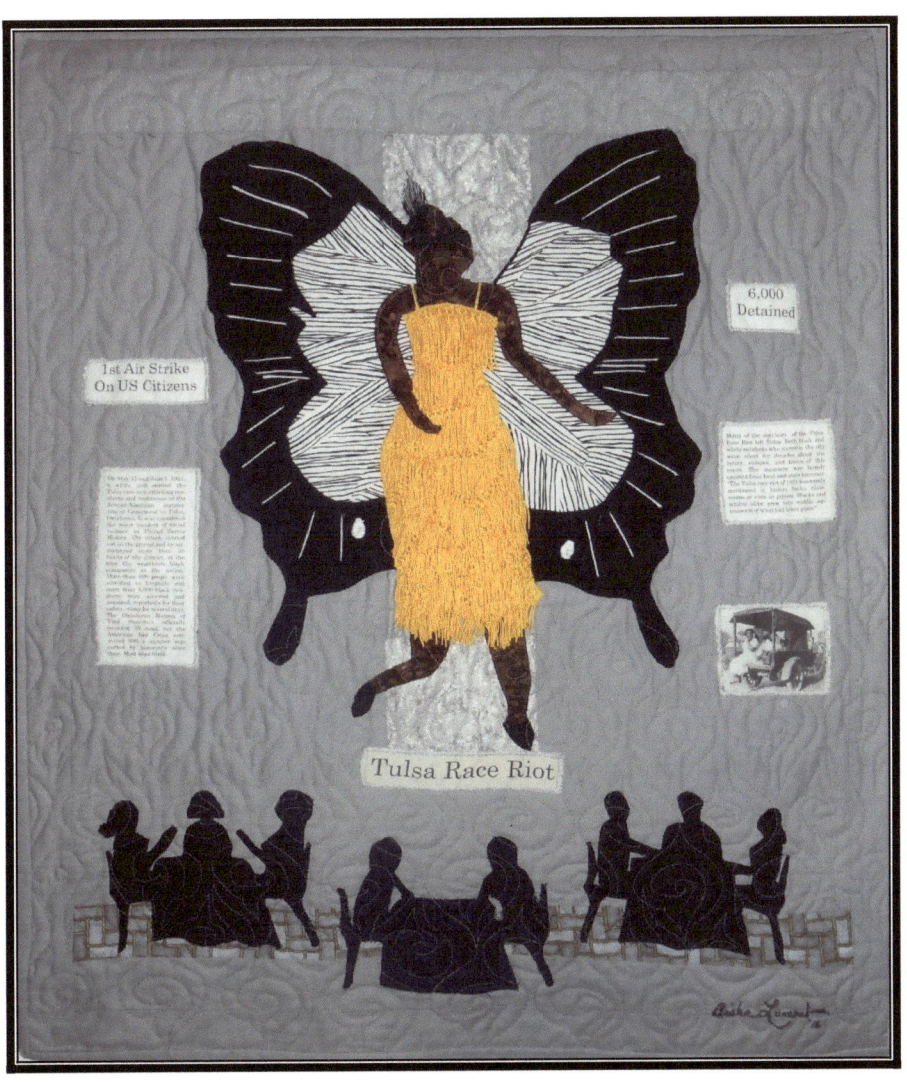

1
1921

"It was a bad one." My dad used to shake his head and say, "it was a bad one" every night when he came in from work. My brother and I would often wonder what was a bad one? What did that mean? IT WAS A BAD ONE.

Eventually, as I lived my life, understood what he meant. I can truly say the summer of the Tulsa Race Riots was a BAD ONE.

It was the way the wind blew in 1921 that made it the worst year of my life. My cousin lived in Tulsa, Oklahoma right inside the Greenwood District and we grew up like sisters. I had the opportunity to visit with her every summer. Greenwood was the highlight of my year, next to Christmas.

My cousin's name was Sally Esther Mae Favors. She was named Sally for our Grandmother and Esther for Uncle Jack's mother. Everyone called her Mae. I called her Cousin Mae. She always asked me to just call her Mae.

Aunt Lula lived in a lovely house. It was a lot different from the cramped quarters we had in Chicago. Her house always smelled like something really good was cooking. She had books in the front room that I was allowed to read. We could sit at the big wooden table in the dining room and read if we were real still. She didn't like us playing in the house. Sometimes in the evenings Aunt Lula would read to me and Cousin Mae. I loved that she read to us because that would give me a chance to learn to pronounce some of the new words I had seen in other books.

Cousin Mae was close to my age, so I thought that was why my mama sent me there in the summer. Cousin Mae and I were close. We shared everything. We didn't really have any secrets that we shared but we pretended to have secrets just so we could whisper about something. We loved whispering and giggling.

We were both skinny little girls with long thin legs. We would run and skip down the sidewalks as the dirt covered our shoes. Some days we would go to the end of the street to see what the Simons were doing. The day they painted the front porch yellow excited Mae so much. She loved the color yellow. She always wanted Aunt Lula to put yellow ribbons on her hair. I didn't have enough hair to put ribbons on so that didn't matter much to me.

Soon we were old enough to walk to the library alone and stop by the drugstore to get ice cream on the way back home. We grew up walking the streets of Tulsa and enjoyed every moment of it.

When we reached our teenage years and finished up school, we had to go to work. Cousin Mae worked in a building in the Greenwood Business District. I was proud to tell my friends that my cousin was learning accounting in an attorney's office. For me, I picked up a little money dancing at the Sunset Café.

Memorial Day weekend in 1921 was unusually warm. It was warm for Chicago anyway, 70's in May is unusual. I wondered if that was some kind of an omen. Old people were always talking about omens, like when all those frogs showed up in Florida.

Looking back I think that warm weather was a sign from the spirit world that people's tempers were boiling over somewhere in the continuum. It was well into the next week before we got word of what had happened in Tulsa. My mom was so worried about Aunt Lula, Uncle Jack and Cousin Mae.

Aunt Lula and my mom were the only two of their siblings left. That fact seemed to make them hold each other closer. Mae and I could tell that the physical distance between them was almost unbearable but they made the most of it.

It was about two weeks before we heard anything from Aunt Lula. It was a simple note saying that she hoped we had some room because she needed a place to live.

My mom was really frantic after she read that note. What about Jack and Mae? Why was she coming alone? What happened to their home? Where was she now? How was she coming? My mom shot off a barrage of questions. I felt the same way but knew to be quiet and let her rant. She was afraid to really know the truth but she knew that soon enough she would have to face what that simple note meant by what it didn't say.

Aunt Lula finally made it by train. She came in so quietly. She was a shell of the person she used to be. My mom shushed me as I was about to open my mouth. So I spoke to Aunt Lula, gave her a little kiss on the cheek and excused myself.

My mom and I waited to hear the story. Aunt Lula had already told us that Uncle Jack and Mae didn't make it. We heard that the whole black area was burned. "Nothing left", Aunt Lula said, "NOTHING." Aunt Lula would get dressed every day and just sit in one place just staring into space.

Then after about a month she said, "it was a full on attack." We stopped what we were doing and listened. She said, "White people were driving down the street shooting anyone they saw. They set buildings and houses on fire. Then the airplanes came and dropped some kind of bombs on our businesses and homes. Some people grabbed their guns and tried to defend us. The flames were everywhere, snapping the crackling wood as structures collapsed. That fire just kept licking the sky with hot reddish orange breath strokes. Jack was shot by the white mob. They just outgunned us. Mae was hurt when the fire spread. I was able to drag her out of the house. Then they detained us for three days. Mae needed medical help but they had burned down the colored hospital. We were not welcome in the white hospital." Aunt Lula said all of that and then sank into the chair as if she were a balloon that all the air had been forced out of.

We were all just weeping. My mom got her nerve up to ask, "Well, what happened to Jack and Mae?" "We buried them and then I left," Aunt Lula responded. She was finally able to release. She sobbed out loud and mom wrapped her arms around her.

Mornings turned into nights and the days flew by. Each day I went to work dutifully. Some days I just sat with Aunt Lula until it was time for me to leave. She was so sad. I wanted to cheer her up but I couldn't. I finally pulled out my yellow dress. Mae sent it to me. I wanted to remember her that night as I danced. Yellow was her favorite color. She said, it made her feel happy like the sunshine.

I may not feel that happiness tonight but I will remember her smile. I love you Mae.

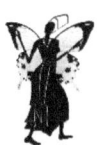

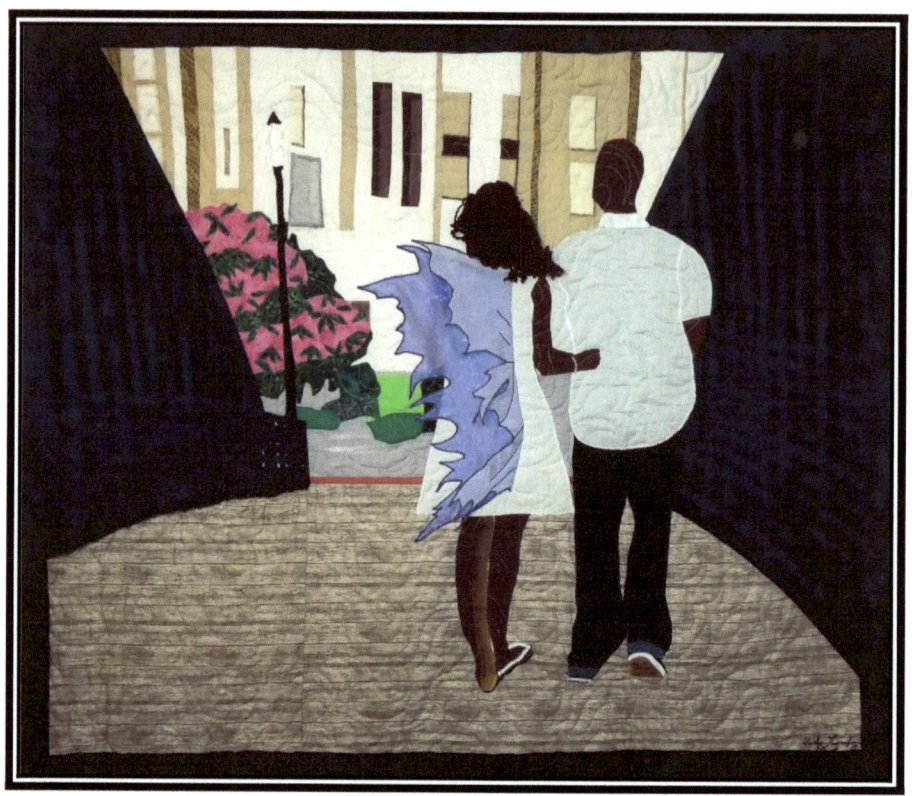

2
2ND ANNIVERSARY

We want a marriage that lasts. Steve and I were pulling out the cards again. Sometimes we make Friday night our snuggle and read the marriage cards time. Steve brought in two glasses of wine and I clutched the magic box.

At our wedding we asked people to give us advice on what makes a marriage last. We put the advice on index cards and made ourselves a little Advice Box. I call it our Magic box because it helps ground us. When things get rocky we pull out the box. Sometimes we pull it out on Friday date night just to reminisce on the happiness we felt at our wedding.

The cards read:

1. Never go to bed arguing or mad with each other.
2. Always listen fully when your spouse is talking.
3. The grass is greener on the other side because they use more manure.
4. An argument/disagreement doesn't mean the marriage is over.
5. Treat your spouse the way you want to be treated.
6. Keep laughter in the marriage.
7. Never fight about money.
8. Don't care who makes the most money
9. Share at least one hobby
10. Have a hobby for yourself
11. Share the chores
12. Believe in something greater than yourself
13. Give some and take some
14. Celebrate the good things (even if they are little things)
15. People who expect more-get more. Have high expectations for each other
16. Stay close to family and friends
17. Remember how you felt when you first fell in love and keep that memory alive.
18. Never argue in front of your children
19. Give each other space
20. Sex is not the most important thing in a marriage but it is up there somewhere near the top of the list.
21. Compromise Compromise Compromise
22. Pledge to never hit each other
23. The man needs friends
24. Show a united front in the presence of the children. Don't let them pit one of you against the other one.

25. Have friends that you do things with.

I remember a time when I was looking for that special someone. Then one day I found a friend. He was the kind of friend that I clicked with right away. I knew what I wanted but didn't think it was possible for me before I met him. One beautiful day I was blessed with a mate, a better half, a special friend for life like a rainbow after a good rain.

It seems like just yesterday when we were dancing at our wedding. The wedding was a big party. The weather cooperated and *almost* everyone that RSVP-ed came.

My dad was cursing everyone that RSVP-ed and didn't come. He said, "they must not understand that we paid for all these seats." Then he would take another sip of his drink. We all knew that it was mostly the drink talking.

Time flies. I look back now over the last two years and wonder how it could have gone by so fast. The next thing I knew I was announcing our baby. It was hard to imagine myself with a baby. I was so happy showing off my little baby bump which grew quickly. Before we knew it, we had a little boy that was getting ready to walk.

We were still celebrating the honeymoon after two years had passed. We were learning more about each other every day. My auntie says it is going to take a lot longer than two years to get to know each other. I guess someday we'll be like that old couple that knows what the other one is thinking and is going to say before they say it.

My ideas about marriage came from watching my parents and my friends' parents. I have to admit that I also got a few ideas about marriage from some TV shows and movies, but some of those ideas didn't seem to match how we lived. I tried to imagine myself making dinner in high heels, a black dress and pearls.

As I watched the different marriages around me, I saw so many things I wanted to do differently. The first thing I wanted to do was figure out how to make it last like my grandparents did. Young marriages had an average life expectancy of three to four years. I wanted a life time if I could get it.

My friends and co-workers think that the wedding ceremony is more important than having a real relationship with the person they are planning to marry. I have seen so many of them put so much stock and money in the one day affair and little to no attention to how they relate to each other.

My cousin told me that he and his wife went to pre-marital counseling for the relationship and to financial workshops. He said, "did you know that 41% of relationships fail because of financial differences." He told me that we should never fight over finances because we have very little control over how much we could realistically make unless we had a printing press. We both laughed.

Now when we walk down the street we still hold hands. I can say for sure that marriage is not as easy as it looks. The first two years have not been all roses but we have honestly worked at it. And we have honestly enjoyed it. We want a marriage that last but that is what everybody wants.

Original photography done by Brian Wagoner of Brian Wagoner Photography Atlanta, Georgia

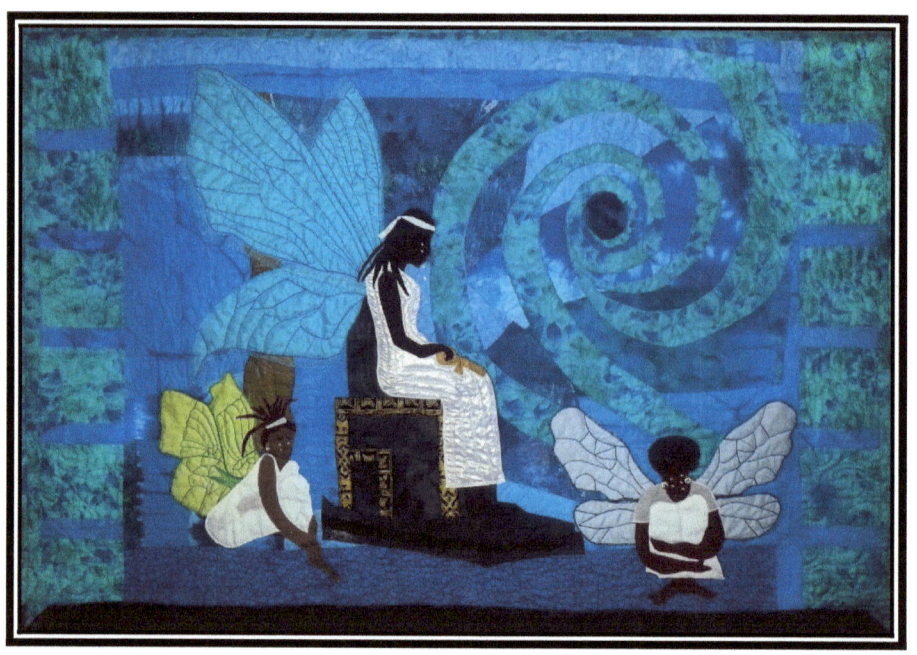

3
AND THE ANGELS CRIED

I walked past the mirror and a voice whispered to me, "and the angels cried." I was lost in thought all day over the senseless deaths of nine people in a church. Nothing in my entire being could find understanding. Nothing inside me could conceive of someone planning and plotting such a heinous crime. Yet it had happened in the victims most sacred place.

I quickly understood what the voice was saying. I knew instantly that the crime was so unthinkable that it even shook the holy beings to their core. What angels? Which angels? What are angels? I first tried to grasp the concept of angels, then tried to grasp what angels looked like when they cried. Thoughts were bouncing all over my brain like ants on a bright red sucker.

Sleep came easier than I thought it would. I only tossed my body for about an hour. The thought of the crying angels followed me into my sleep and invaded my dreams. I found myself standing on a cubic block before an ever changing background of shapes that I tried to comprehend before they changed again. Then I fixed my eyes on the spinning spiral. My eyes could follow the spinning. It was soothing. I felt as though I was a baby being rocked to sleep in my mother's arms. But I was already asleep, I thought.

As the undulating spiral turned I could clearly see three figures seated before me. They were all dressed in white with enormous wings. The wings caught my attention even though the light around them was blinding. The beings looked like me. The angels explained that they are light beings that merely reflect the present physical state of the onlooker, therefore, each person's vision of angels looks like them. That explained the hair and the hue of their skin. I felt safe with them.

The trickling sound of water from a spring that I could not see tickled my ears. I loved that sound. The angels tears flowed with the same ebb as a stream. I was so busy soaking in the environment that I allowed the angels to fade into the background. The water was talking to me like a song that I knew but could not translate into my own language. The healing had already begun.

They cried. I cried. Then names and faces of the victims floated in and out of the spinning surroundings. A bright light engulfed them and whisked them away. The spiral, the tears, the running water and the light all acted as healing agents. Soothing and waving over us. Us? I had become one with the Emmanuel Nine. I was spinning in the light with them. I touched them and they reached out to me.

Before I knew it, we were spinning and spinning around in the light. Then they separated from me and floated away on a soft puff of air. The Emmanuel Nine became nine little balls of light. They flew around as they merged into the light behind the spiral. The brilliance of the light hurt my eyes.

I felt heavy, very heavy. The sounds became softer and softer until I didn't hear them anymore. The light faded as well. I sank into a heavy darkness and woke myself up by my own snoring.

I finally understood why the Angels cried. Their tears were really a part of the healing process. The Angels tears were to our spirit as rain is to the forest--just pure healing.

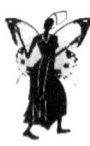

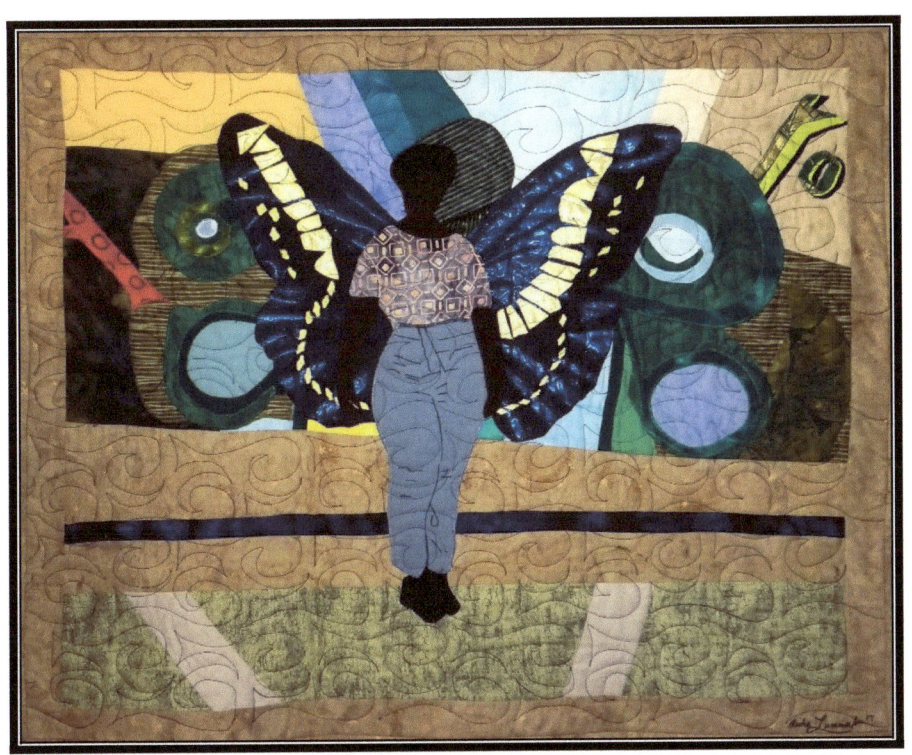

4
CLAUDIA

As a matter of fact, we dark skinned people are beautiful in our own right, I said out loud for anyone listening to hear. I often had to straighten people about that fact.

One day a young man said, "You are really cute for a dark skinned girl." Several things went through my mind but I didn't let them out of my mouth. I looked closely only to find that the person staring at me had no idea that what he thought was a compliment was really an insult. My brain went through a litany of responses. Many of them unkind and inappropriate. Instead I said, "I am sure there is a compliment in there somewhere because my father is cute for a dark skinned person too." The answer was a little sarcastic but it was okay because it went over his head.

I walked on by and tried to remember the first time I was aware of my complexion. A short trip around my memory bank brought up a vivid memory. Some new neighbors had moved in across the street from us. The family included two girls that were our age. One girl was my complexion and her sister was several shades lighter like my sister. I don't know why that difference struck me. My sister and I had the same complexion difference and I had not noticed it. As a matter of fact, our situation didn't faze me until I started getting taunted.

We spent as many hours playing with those girls as daylight would allow. Sometimes on Friday nights we were allowed to play long after the sun had set. Catching fireflies was our specialty. Some Saturdays the Ice Cream Man would come by and we would beg for money to buy an ice cream cone.

One night late the house across the street caught on fire. I found out about it the next morning. I slept right through the loud sound of the firetruck. And just like that our neighbors were gone but they had opened my eyes to the differences in skin color.

So that brings me back to being cute in spite of my dark skin. I wasn't always so clear and proud of my skin color. My father said that his teacher told the class that it was their duty to lighten the race by marrying someone lighter than themselves. Absurd! I didn't hear anything as blatant but the subtle racism was ever present. For instance, only the girls with a certain skin color got invited to eat at a certain table at lunch.

My parents decided to stop the madness. They taught us about loving ourselves and to be proud of our history. One day I rushed home with icy tears on my face and my scarf floating behind me. I put my coat and my books in a heap on the floor. I rushed in and shouted, Mother, the children were all teasing me about being dark! They called me Boot Black and laughed, I said. She said calmly, "Well you know that is not your name, don't you?" Yes but they laughed at me. "Do you still know that you are special?," she asked. Yes I said, even more perplexed. Well when your father comes home he will tell you a story. Not another story, I yelled inside my head. He was always telling me a story.

When father came home, he let me sit in his lap although I was way too big to sit in his lap. "I hear you had a little trouble at school," he said. Yes I whimpered. Well let me tell you a story. I knew that was coming. "Long long ago in a land far away that is now called Africa, the people who lived there called themselves the children of the sun. They were great people with a successful government that included Kings and Queens. They had aqueduct systems which created a way to water the crops. They were astronomers, mathematicians, scientists, and physicians.

"One day some people came that did not look like them. They brought goods to trade and a different kind of religion. Everything they shared was coupled with a religious lesson. The people of the sun grew comfortable with the new people. The new people settled in and built fortresses on the edge of the water right in their communities. As they traveled back and forth to their homeland, more and more people came back with them. What the people of the sun did not know was that at night- under the cloak of darkness they marched groups of people to their fortress. They loaded them onto ships and carted them away. Eventually, the settlers just started an all-out attack on the people of the sun and started taking people away in large numbers by force," he said. Oh boy, I felt like I had opened a can of worms.

How long was this story going to be? "Do you know where the people were taken?" he asked. I made a wild guess, to the United States. "Yes that is kind of right, only it was the original 13 colonies at that time. They were also taken to South America and the Caribbean Islands." But what does that have to do with us hating our dark skin?, I asked.

"Because that was the most obvious difference between the people of the sun and the settlers. The settlers had white skin. They used it to make themselves seem superior and the dark people seem inferior. We as a people were systematically trained to disdain our skin color, the darker the skin-the more disdain. We were taught to call each other names like black, darkie, nigger, nigga, blackie and other names that corresponded to being dark skinned. Those were the names the settlers used when they spoke of us and to us. Your skin didn't necessarily have to be dark to feel insulted by being called black. No one wanted to be called black because that was an insult.

"Calling each other those names strengthened the idea of self-hatred. It let the world know that we had bought into the idea that we are less than others because of our skin pigmentation. The fact that many of our people think that they have turned the meaning of the word around by using it affectionately just shows that the self-hatred strategy is successful. I have heard those same people who swear they are using the "N" word lovingly-use it with disdain and contempt for their fellow dark skinned people, which in turn means that they hate themselves as well," he explained.

I got it. It was a lot to take in but I got the jest of it. As time went on, I began to understand it better. The story was constantly reinforced in our home. We learned to be proud that we came from a great people who were dark skinned and there is nothing wrong with being dark skinned. As a matter of fact, we are cute in our own right.

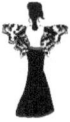

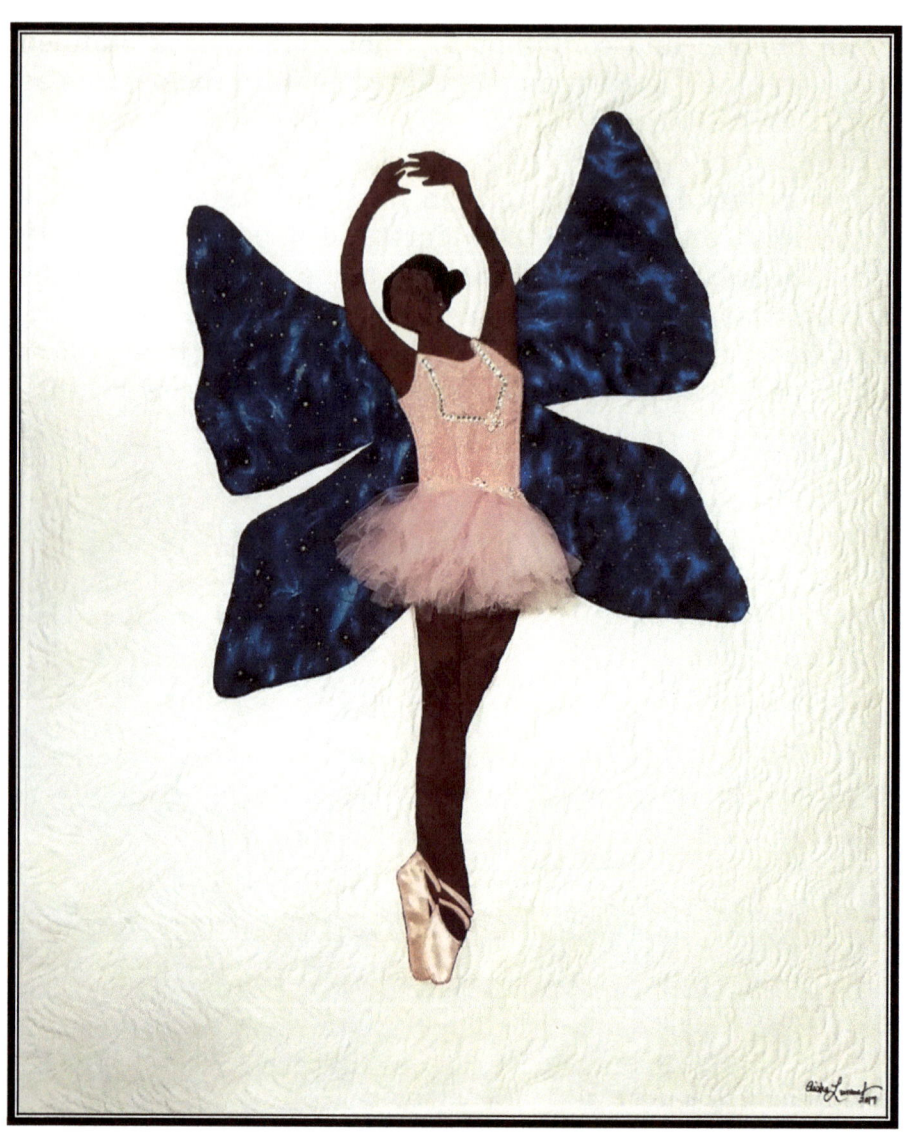

5
CONFIDENCE!

My mother named me Confidence because she had none. I was exceptionally small at birth. My mother said that I filled out in no time flat. She said that love fattened me up and made me strong. I'd heard of people naming their children after cars that they would like to own, like Mercedes or Porsche. I was the first person that was named after a feeling as far as I could tell.

Mother would tell me that she wanted more for me, a better life she would say. I often wondered exactly what that meant. She would laugh and say give me a hug my little confidence. Then she would sing my favorite song. I loved to hear her sing. Her voice could be so soft and melodic, then she could switch and reach low for a note that sounded like moaning from pain.

I knew I was special between her singing and my dad spinning me around. I would spin and then dance. He smiled the biggest grin ever when I danced. Then I would beg him to twirl me again.

My dad would get really upset when he heard my mother sing. Sometimes he would hit her and tell her that no one wanted to hear her sing. Most of the time after that he would drink. I wanted to drink with him. Mother   said those drinks were only for adults not like the juice she would give me. She would then take me away and we would leave him watching TV and drinking.

Dad was never mean to me and I felt so confused when he was mean to mother. When I was really little, he would let me sit on his lap and stroke his beard. I loved him so much, especially when he would twirl me and tell me to dance. He loved my dancing as much as I loved him.

When I danced, I could feel the music inside of me. The music told me which way to move and dad egged me on.

Then one day after my twelfth birthday, we moved away from him. Mother and I went to stay with her parents. I went to a new school and mother enrolled me into some dance classes. She said that dance was surely a way to find my confidence.

My dance teacher said that I took to dance like a fish takes to water. I loved to dance and I didn't mind working hard on the routines. At first I took for granted that I could easily follow the steps and I had a hard time understanding why others could not do it. I realized that each one of us had our own special gifts and mine was dance.

Every now and then I twirl around and think of my dad. He used to spin me around and I felt so happy. I missed having him in my life. I didn't dare say that to my mom because she seemed so happy without him. At least that is what I thought. Mother would sing all the time. She sang all around the house. She sang when she did the dishes, folded the clothes and cooked the meals. Her happy singing would make me forget that longing feeling I had for dad.

Every now and then mother would drive a different route home. She drove by a place where homeless men would lean against the wall near the underpass of the bridge. She pretended not to see Dad there and so I pretended that I didn't see him either. He looked so tired and worn down. She never spoke about him but she drove there religiously each month.

Early one Friday morning I had a sinking feeling in my stomach. I couldn't understand that because Friday was always my favorite day of the week. I went through the day looking for that joy that usually followed me but there was a gloom hanging over my head. It felt like a little cloud had positioned itself directly over my head.

Mother was waiting on me when I arrived home. She

looked down and out. I rushed in and asked her what was wrong. Her head was down and she spoke slowly. Your dad died today. WHAT?, I screamed. WHAT!!!! This could not be happening. I haven't interacted with him for years and now he is gone. How dare he die before I got to see him again? The little cloud over my head released its water. My mother held me tight and we cried.

I decided to keep him in my heart when I danced. I twirled and he was there, smiling just like he did when I was a little girl. I was his little girl and in a roundabout way because of him, I had plenty of confidence.

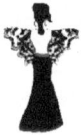

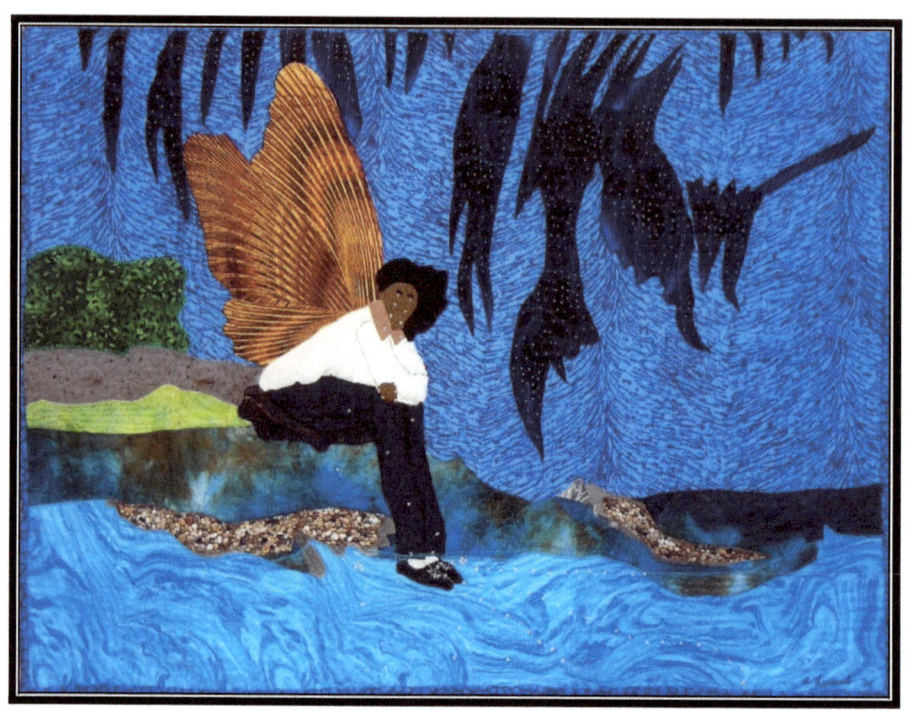

6
CRY ME A RIVER

"A mother should never have to bury her own child." I am a member of a sacred club. It is a club that no mother wants to belong to. It is a heartbreaking and heart wrenching group. It's not a real structured group with walls, rules or goals. We all just simply want the pain to stop.

The years tick by and the hole in my heart never heals. I tell people that I am ok but I may never really be ok. I am coping but I'm not ok. I'm going through the motions like a well-oiled machine. The big tears don't show on the outside anymore but they pour inside. And in my quiet moments, the silent slow tears flow.

My son was the love of my life but this society accused him of being violent, just another angry black man. This society says that we are monsters, murderers, thieves and lazy. They make every attempt to show badly through the media by only focusing on reports of us committing crimes. You would think that there is nothing good happening in our lives. That depiction of us is so confusing to me.

If we had robbed a continent of its' people, beat and whipped them, enslaved them, raped the women, impregnated the women and sold the children, hung the people from trees, hung them from bridges, drug them behind horses, drug them behind trucks, took the people from their homes in the middle of the night at gunpoint and killed them on railroad tracks, shot up their homes, burned crosses in their yard, bombed their churches, shot people in church during bible study, destroyed people's lives by declaring war on them after dishonoring treaties and then stole their indigenous land, then I would understand why society claims we are savages. But we have not done that, we have not done any of that. We have merely tried to survive in a hostile environment, an environment that is hostile to us. We have learned how to act from the dominant culture and we've been persecuted for it.

My son was an unarmed black man shot by the police. My best friends' son was shot by some black intruders in a home invasion. My other best friends' son was killed during a carjacking. My friends' son was shot by a man claiming to be on Neighborhood watch. My cousins son was choked to death by a group of white policeman. My aunties' son was shot right on the street by a black man. Another friends son was shot in the park by police who thought his toy gun was real. My neighbors daughter's boyfriend was shot in a car by the police in front of her and her child. Eight of my girlfriends sons were shot driving while black. One of them was shot because he didn't have his license with him. Some young black kids were shot because they were playing the music too loud. I know a lady whose son was naked when the police shot him. And another mother's son was rolled up in a gym mat. The list goes on. Young black men are being killed at an alarming rate by policeman and by other black people. So disheartening.

Excuse me please. I feel the silent tears coming. He was stopped for a missing tail light. When he asked the officer why he was stopped, the officer said, "I'll ask the questions." The next thing we know is that he was drug from the car, handcuffed, and beaten. They didn't take him to the hospital. He just laid there and died. The coroner said he had broken ribs which punctured his lungs.

My son was a chubby little baby with a hearty laugh. I loved to tickle him. He walked at one years old and went to school at six. He excelled in high school and became an outstanding young man and father. I have asked why a million times. Now I try to explain to his daughter that her father is not coming home. I can tell by the look on her face that she doesn't understand what I am saying. Hell, I don't understand it either.

It is not only sons that are taken. Daughters have gone away as well. It hurts the same. Will it ever stop? So I cry a river for all of those mothers who have lost their children.

The unfortunate thing about my crying a river is that it

doesn't console me, doesn't bring my son back, nor has it changed the state of the nation. I don't know if I'll ever stop crying these tears but I know that love will eventually triumph.

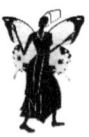

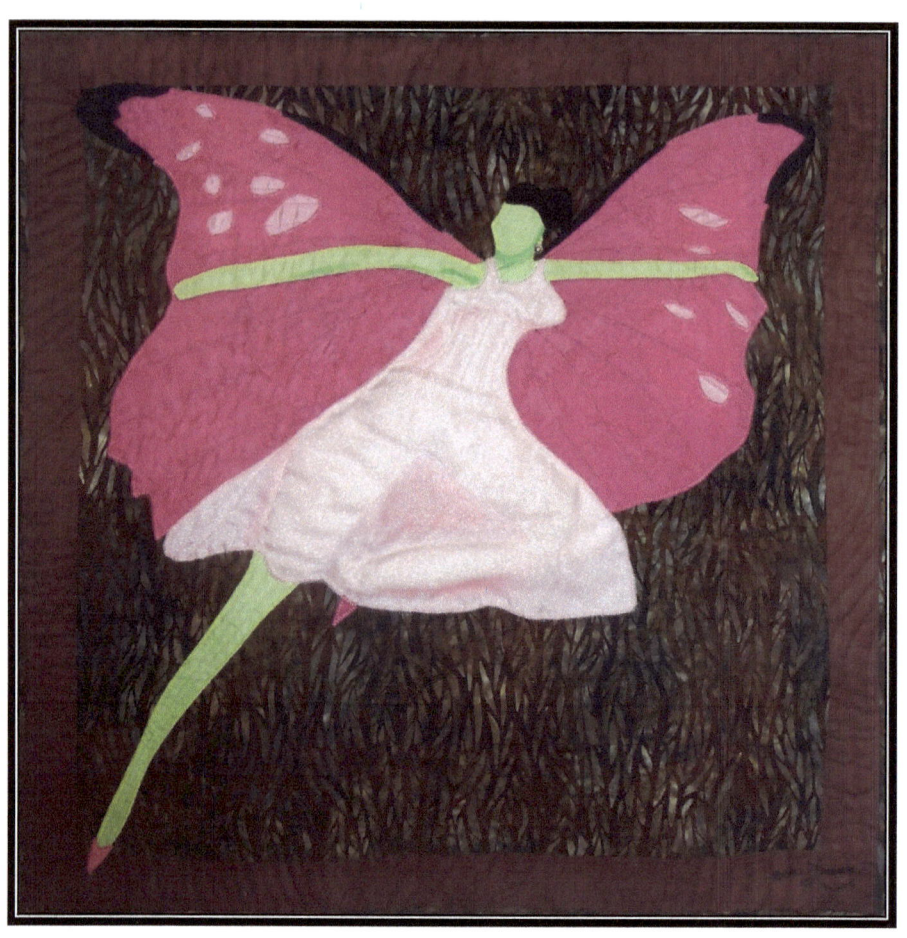

7
FLYING BALLERINA

Front steps are no place to start your life. I was left on the steps by my mother. That is what the birth records say. I was shipped from one foster home to another. What I learned at one place, I had to unlearn in the next. I loved to sit in the corner and read. Sometimes I would hide in the closet to be alone. Whenever I was allowed to go outside, I would run. I could have been a ballerina but I loved to run more than dance. A lady came to the home and taught ballet once a week but I wanted to run. I could run until I fell out on the ground with exhaustion. Running took the empty feeling away, at least for a little while. Sometimes when I run with the wind blowing across my face, I feel like I am flying. I chuckle to myself that I could have been a flying ballerina.

I didn't want to be a loner but I didn't know how not to be. One foster home was pretty nice. I met a girl there named Carol. She would make me laugh. We read together and played outside together. The house was really nice and clean. The parents were so good to us. We always had enough to eat and good clothes. Carol taught me how to be friends. We didn't stay at that home long.

Things were always changing around me from place to place until that wonderful day that I received my own forever family.

Mrs. Brown walked into the center wearing a navy blue suit, a big hat and high heels. Mr. Brown followed behind, after he put out his cigarette. They looked like a good family to me and I was so overjoyed to be going home with them.

When I got to the Brown household, Carol was there. She too had been shifted around a lot. I was beaming to see her but she didn't look so happy. I would soon find out why.

Later that night Carol said, "I am so glad you are here but this is not a good place. You'll see." Mrs. Brown had a washing and ironing business. She needed workers. I was ushered into the team and made to wash and iron alongside Carol. Carol showed me how to work faster.

We worked all day and sometimes into the night. We

worked every day after school and all day on the weekend. If we didn't do it just like Mrs. Brown wanted it, she would beat us.

Mrs. Brown's son played chess against himself all the time. In between his games, he spent his days telling us what to do and reporting to his mom about what we were and were not doing.

After a couple of months Carol asked, "has Mr. Brown approached you yet?" What do you mean approached me?, I responded. "He likes young girls. It is just a matter of time before he slips into your bed" she said.

Not again, I thought. A forever family was supposed to be a good place, a safe place. From that day on I started watching Mr. Brown. I didn't see any sign of what Carol said. He started giving me candy and buying little extra gifts for me. He liked me, I thought.

My ninth birthday was a big affair. I had never been so happy or felt so special. Mrs. Brown made a cake for me and invited a few children from the neighborhood over. Mr. Brown bought me a special doll. It was not the new kind of doll that looked like me. It was the kind that I wanted. The doll had long blonde hair that I could comb and light skin. She looked like I wanted to look. I loved my new doll.

Shortly after that ninth birthday, Mr. Brown started coming to my bed. I was so confused because he was hurting me but he liked me. He would always bring me something special the next day.

It went on for about six years. Then it stopped as suddenly has it had started. When I went to high school, Mr. Brown faded back into the background of my life.

Mrs. Brown had changed as well. I missed whatever had brought about the change but I welcomed it.

I joined the track team in high school. The coach said he had never seen anyone as young as me with such good form. I instinctively knew how to run like the wind. He didn't know that I needed to run, to feel free. I loved the feel of the breeze on my skin as I sped around the track. I loved to feel as though my body was trying to keep up with my legs.

I went through several bad relationships before Ben found me. I had totally stopped looking for a boyfriend when this nice gentleman asked to hold the door for me. I know there is no such thing as love at first sight but something happened. I looked in his eyes and knew that he was the one.

I kept telling myself that it was his kindness that I wanted and needed. Then I realized that it was alright to want, need and be treated with kindness. Ben helped me develop a new attitude, a new sense of myself.

So after the birth of our baby, I may have the opportunity to run again. I don't dance, I run.

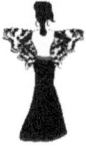

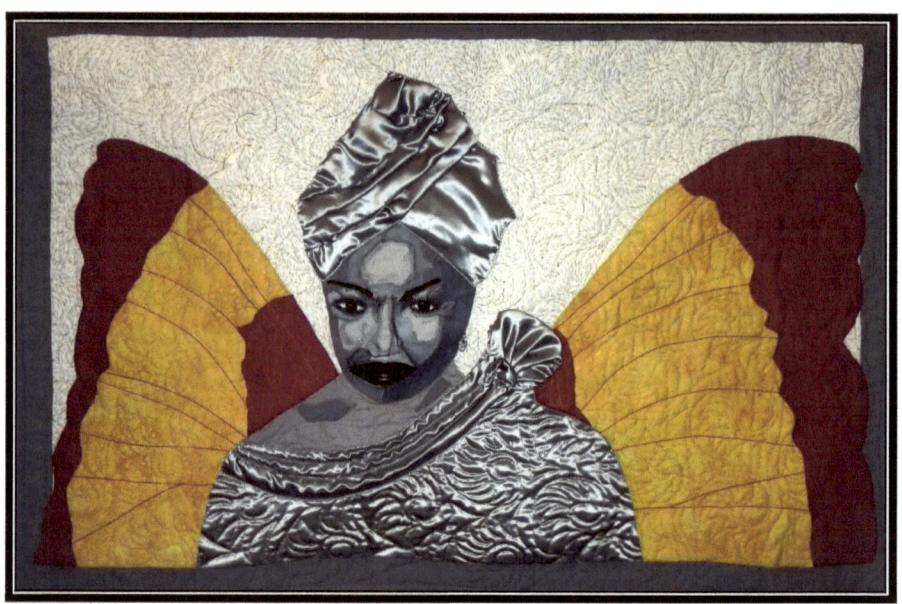

8
GODDAM

When I wrote Mississippi Goddam, I was feeling the constant weight of blatant racism. It was like a fire boiling inside of me. It boiled up and up until it filled my body. It exploded in my head, smoke came out my ears and steam came out my nose. The only relief from the fire was the tears that flowed from my eyes.

I was watching the television as demonstrators were herded into jails in Birmingham, Alabama for challenging segregation. Then I saw the National Guard called to allow two Black students to attend the University of Alabama. I remembered being mistreated because of my skin color when I was young. To this day I have not been able to understand racism. No human being (and we all are) should have to suffer because of something that was given to them naturally.

Have you ever heard of the straw on the camel's back?

Well the load was getting heavier and heavier. I kept telling myself that I was not going to let it get me to the breaking point.

It was a hot day in June when I heard about the police brutality down in the Delta. Some movement activists were returning from Citizenship School training in South Carolina. They were brutally beaten by law enforcement in the Winona, Mississippi jail after they tried to eat at the bus depot's white lunch counter. Three teenagers, SCLC organizer Annell Ponder, SNCC field secretary Lawrence Guyot, and former sharecropper and voting rights worker Fannie Lou Hamer. Ms. Ponder was beaten so severely that her whole face was swollen. I heard that she motioned the reporter to lean in close and through her swollen lips she whispered, "FREEDOM." I said, my kind of woman with a fighting spirit. Ms. Hamer suffered permanent damage from the attack and that saddened me tremendously. I said, Mississippi Goddam!

Music kept me from being too depressed. I kept my engagements and performed as usual but the struggle for equality stayed heavy on my heart. Then Medgar Evers was killed at his home in Jackson, Mississippi.

Every time I thought about Medgar's shooting, I would say, Mississippi goddam. That was a really restless time. I found myself saying goddam the whole summer. We didn't know what could or would happen next. The killing was so unthinkable and horrific, that we were just holding our breath.

A little over a week after Medgar's death, three Freedom Summer workers were missing·· Michael Schwerner, James Chaney and Andrew Goodman. Two weeks later on August 4, their bullet riddled bodies were found in a dam. Mississippi goddam.

September brought my focus back to Alabama when some terribly misguided beings bombed the 16th Street Baptist Church in Birmingham, killing four little girls. I didn't call those people monsters, although it would have been easy to do. Who else would put fifteen sticks of dynamite under the girls' restroom or under a building knowing that people would inhabit it? That act made my blood boil. I called their names out loud - Addie Mae Collins , Carole Robertson, Cynthia Wesley and Denise McNair. I felt the heartbreak of the families and the community. It was the third bombing in Birmingham in 11 days. I bit my tongue and said Alabama goddam under my breath.

Children were marching and being detained in many places in the south. It was so disheartening to hear that children were in the jails singing freedom songs.

I was still in and out of performances but my mind stayed on freedom. I could not get the movement out of my mind. My cousin called to tell me about the things going on around her. She said, "Honey there are all kinds of legal battles, protests, sit-ins, marches and boycotts. We are trying to push the federal government to outlaw segregation." I couldn't sleep thinking that someone in Tennessee might be next. I prayed that nothing would happen to my cousin.

The whole struggle had me questioning the existence of God. I asked, how could God just let so many horrible things happen to us. Where is God? Two contradictory answers came to mind, 1) God will move when the time is right or 2) God helps those who help themselves. Were we supposed to wait on God to change things or were we supposed to make a move ourselves?

Late in October a friend stopped by. I went right to work telling him how I was feeling. I poured us a drink and never missed a beat with my rant. He sipped and listened intently. Then said, "take it slow." TAKE IT SLOW, I snapped. What do you mean take it slow? I wanted to slap the taste of that drink out of his mouth. He said some things come in their own due time. I took a real deep breath, looked straight in his eyes and said, when do you think our time is due? When we were picking cotton or maybe when we were fighting for our own freedom in the civil war or better yet when our churches were being bombed?

My friend didn't know what to say. He was obviously repeating something he had heard without thinking it through. Well I had thought it through, a lot. I couldn't see going slow as an answer. Sun up to sun down work was not taking it slow. Building the white house from the ground up was not taking it slow. Building city after city all over this country was not taking it slow.

It was my thought then and I still think it now. We have to stand up and be counted. It is time we stood up for our own freedom because nobody is going to give it to us.

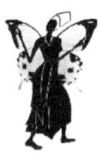

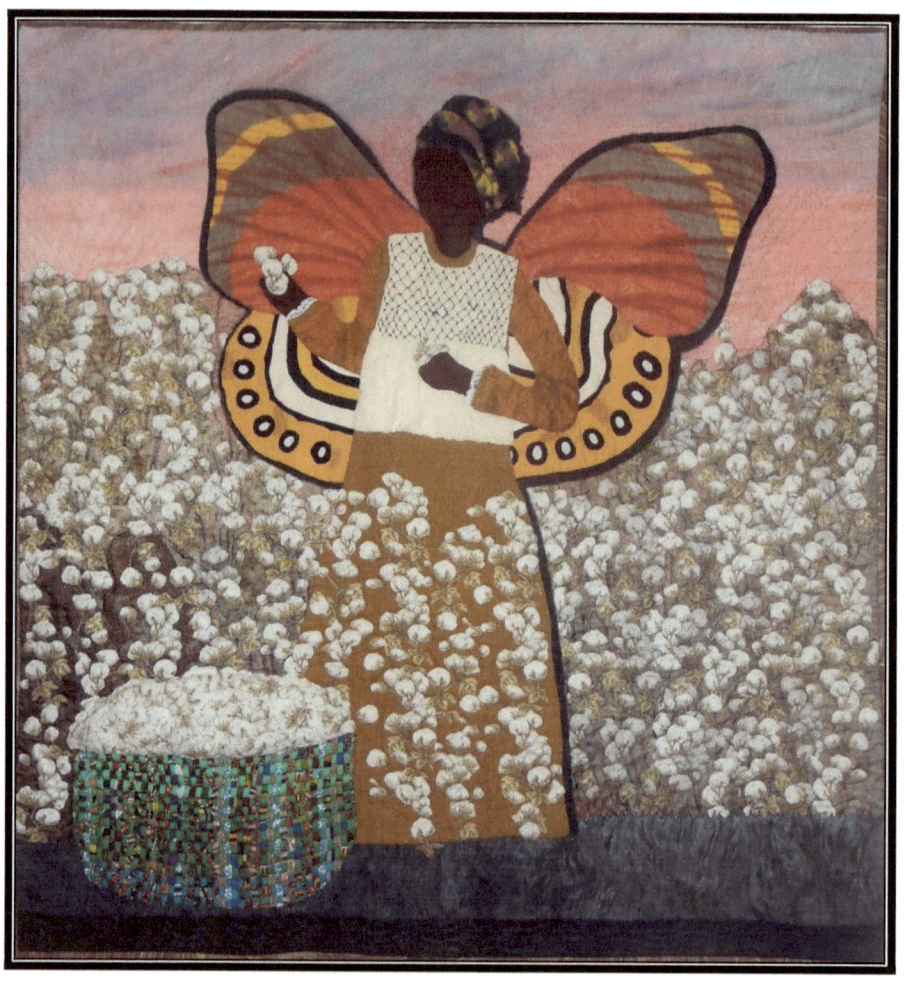

9
HIGH COTTON

Dese days is long but da nights is longer. When we gits thru workin' in da field we has ta work at home ta git ready fa ta morrow. It's lack a wheel that goes round and round. We wake up 'fo day in the moanin' so we can be in da field by da time da sun come up. Da cotton is high dis year but it ain't always dis high. Some years it is back breakin' work ta bend down ta git all dat cotton. If I has ta lack dis cotton, I got ta lack da high cotton bess.

After da long day, I drags mysef in and makes us some supper. I put a pot of beans over da fireplace 'fo we left dis moanin'. Dat way dey can cook a little while da fi' dies down. Now I gots ta git the fi' going again fa da night and so it can cook da beans da res of da way and da bread. Sometimes I has sweet potatoes dat I can cook in da fi' but not taday. Jes beans and cone bread taday.

I'm gon try ta git a lil time on dat quilt I been makin' while James gather up some mo' fi' wood. Iz tied but da quilting lets me settle my mind down. I thanks 'bout freedom when I sew da pieces tagether. I thanks 'bout freedom a lot. Freedom fa me and fa James and da boys.

Massa Charlie thanks if he keeps us busy den we won't have time ta thank 'bout freedom. He thanks if he beats us, we be too scared ta thank 'bout freedom. We don't let on dat wese always thankin' bout freedom. Da harder we work, da mo' we thanks 'bout it. Sometimes in da fields somebody git ta thankin 'bout it kinda hard and dey starts wit a low moan. Somma my cousins start ta moan too. Umm um umm hum. Um hum hum hummmm. Way down in da rows dey start real low an soft wit da words · "In da moanin' I'm goin' home. I'm goin home in da moanin." Den we chimes in an sez, "In da moanin I'm goin' home, I'm goin' home in da moanin." Da overseer thanks we sangin 'bout goin ta heaven like dey teach us in da church, but we is thankin' 'bout freedom. Sho is. We is sangin, workin, and thankin' 'bout freedom.

We sang and work, den we sangs some mo'. We gits a lil sumpin teat when da sun gits high o'er head and den we works some mo'. Mandy's sweet voice starts it up again wit· "Swing low sweet chariot, comin fo ta carry me home. Da dream of flyin' away from all dis sufferin' and all dis hard work is strong in our hearts. Sangin' makes da day go by lil easier.

My susta got sold off ta anotha plantation lass year. It so hard ta go on wit out her. It waz after Massa Charlie beat her. It broke me inside ta watch dat whip crack across her back. He say she was a problem cuz she don't do what he say. Massa don't lao us ta be proud but seems lack she jes couldn't hep it. She had her own mind 'bout hersef.

An Iz 'fraid dey gone sell one of my boys next. When Massa Charlie needs money an da crops don't do well, he sells off somebody. He thanks we is livestock lack da chickens or cows an don't have no feelins.

James talks ta me 'bout runnin' but he don't want ta leave wit out me and da boys. I thanks Massa knows dat havin' a family 'ill keep some men from runnin'. Massa always happy when someone wants ta jump da broom, cuz our chilluns add ta da count of peoples he owns.

Ain't no family, no beatin', no hangin', can keep some folks from runnin'. Some would rather take dey chances cause dey say dis is no life. Me and James is keepin on fa our future chilluns chillun, cuz dats what da people who came befo us did fa us.

Some dez I stand in da mist of all dat cotton as da sun sets low in da evening and thank I could jes fly way.

[*Translation*]

These days are long but the nights are longer. When we get through working in the field we have to work at home to get ready for tomorrow. It's like a wheel that goes around and around. We wake up before day in the morning so we can be in the field by the time the sun comes up. The cotton is high this year but it ain't always this high. Some years it is back breaking work to bend down to get all of that cotton. If I have to like this cotton, I got to like high cotton best.

After the long day, I drag myself in and make us some supper. I put a pot of beans over the fireplace before we left this morning. That way they can cook a little while the fire dies down. Now I got to get the fire going again for the night and so it can cook the beans the rest of the way and the bread. Sometimes I have sweet potatoes that I can cook in the fire but not today. Just beans and corn bread today.

I'm going to try and get a little time on that quilt I've been making while James gathers up some more fire wood. I am tired but the quilting lets me settle my mind down. I think about freedom when I sew the pieces together. I think about freedom a lot. Freedom for me and for James and the boys.

Master Charlie thinks if he keeps us busy then we won't have time to think about freedom. He thinks if he beats us, we will be too scared to think about freedom. We don't let on that we're always thinking about freedom. The harder we work, the more we think about it. Sometimes in the fields somebody gets to thinking about it kind of hard and they starts with a low moan. Some of my cousins start to moan too. Umm um umm hum. Um hum hum hummmm. Way down in the rows they start real low an soft with the words - "In da moanin' I'm goin' home. I'm goin home in da moanin." Then we chime in and say, "In da moanin I'm goin' home, I'm goin' home in da moanin." The overseer thinks we are singing about going to heaven like they teach us in the church, but we is thinking about freedom. Sure is. We is singing, working, and thinking about freedom.

We sing and work, then we sing some more. We get a little something to eat when the sun gets high overhead and then we work some more. Mandy's sweet voice starts it up again with- "Swing low sweet chariot, coming forth to carry me home. The dream of flying away from all of this suffering and all of this hard work is strong in our hearts. Singing makes the day go by a little easier.

My sister got sold off to another plantation last year. It so hard to go on without her. It was after Master Charlie beat her. It broke me inside to watch that whip crack across her back. He say she was a problem because she didn't do what he say. Master don't allow us to be proud but seems like she just couldn't help it. She had her own mind about herself.

And I'm afraid they [are] going [to] sell one of my boys next. When Master Charlie needs money and the crops don't do well, he sells off somebody. He thinks we are livestock like the chickens or cows and don't have no feelings.

James talks to me about running [away] but he don't want to leave without me and the boys. I think Master knows that having a family will keep some men from running, Master [is] always happy when someone wants to jump the broom, because our children add to the count of peoples he owns.

Ain't no family, no beating, no hanging, can keep some from running. Some would rather take their chances cause they say this is no life. James and I are keeping on for our future children's children. That's what the people who came before us did for us.

Some days I stand in the mist of all that cotton as the sun

sets low in the evening and think I could just fly away.

The Process

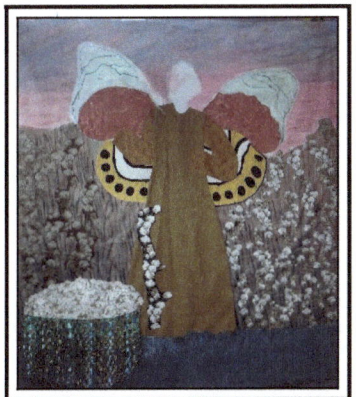 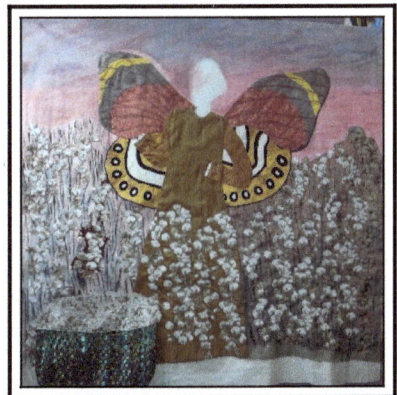

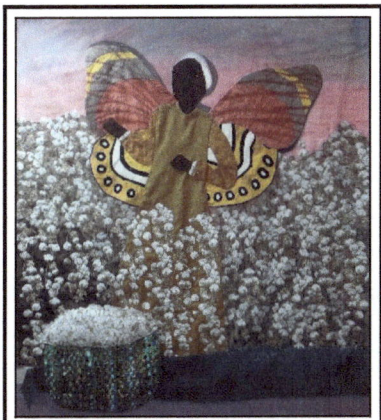 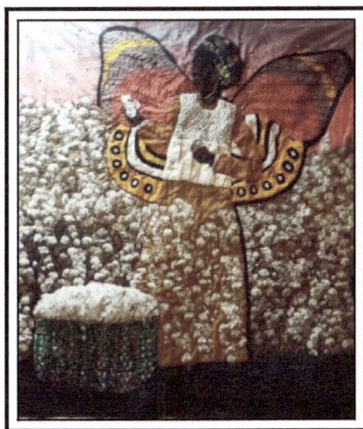

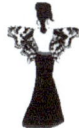

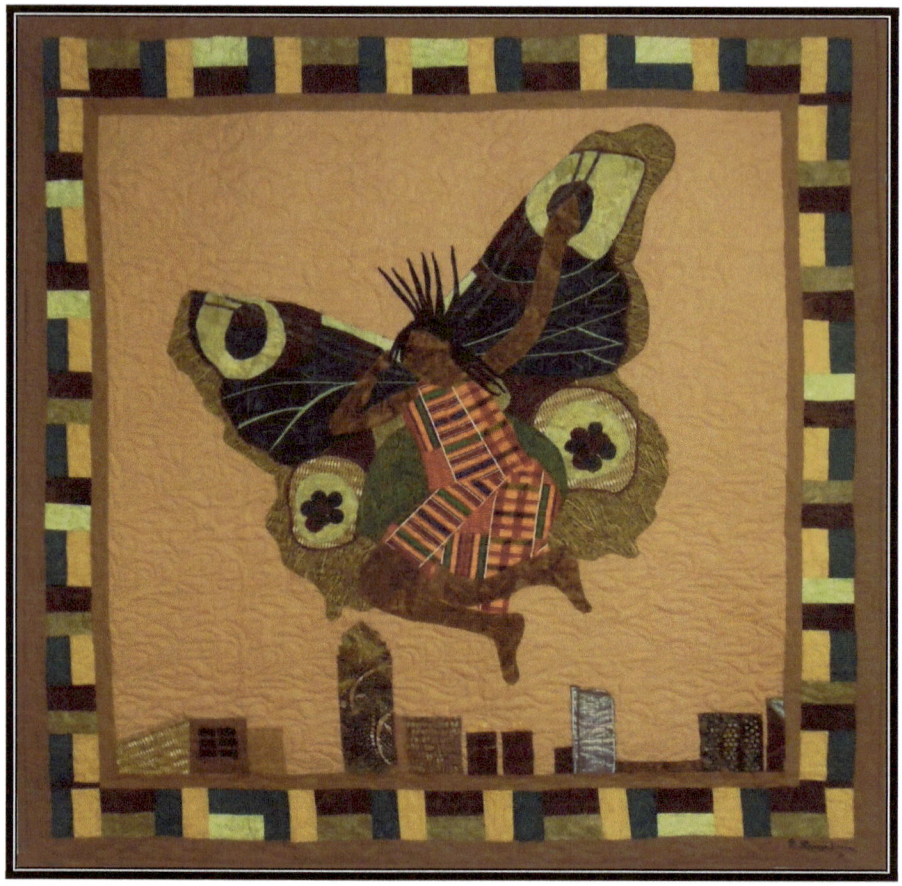

10
LEAP

I came to the city from a small country town determined to hold on to my smile. I read a lot of books about people in different and wonderful places around the world when I was a young girl. I couldn't wait to get out and explore some of those places. Bright lights and big city certainly had gone to my head. I told everyone that I was moving to the city as soon as I turned eighteen. I would be legally old enough to live on my own. Yes the city was the place for me.

My friends warned me about moving to the city. They had no such aspirations. Home was the best place to be and they did not want to leave. One of my classmates said that I would be back soon to live with my parents. I vowed that would never happen and worked doubly hard to make sure it did not.

The city proved to be all I thought it would. It was fast and exciting. Something to do all the time and somewhere to go whenever you wanted. And the list of night clubs, WOW, I loved going to the night clubs. I wasn't a big drinker but I was a dance fanatic. I loved to dance in the club with the booming music. I could lose myself in the music.

I worked hard and spent almost every penny I made. I thought new shoes were the best thing in the world. I had never had more than two pair of shoes at any given time in my life. I bought green shoes, orange shoes, red shoes, blue shoes, gold shoes and many many black shoes. I had no real idea of saving for rainy days.

I had a car and drove fast like young people. I had a lot of places that I wanted to go and thought I had to get there as fast as I could. Life was good and I couldn't imagine anything different. That was until I wrecked my car. The awakening was rude and fast.

I was a smart cookie. I could calculate money in my head a lot faster than I could realistically make it. Since I was so young and inexperienced, I had no idea of all the other factors involved in calculating one's future.

I started selling Ruby Kate Cosmetics. I had my calculator smoking with the projected money I was going to make. I could see it clearly. I hated my job anyway, so I quit. I just knew working Ruby Kate full time was the best way to go. I was well on my way. Jetting here and there, setting up appointments and doing demonstrations. My little hand-held calculator did not tell me that I needed a car to do what I was doing. And why should it? I had a car so that was not a consideration. Yes I had a car one day and the next day, I did not. In my foolish mind, I thought I could keep my business going on the bus.

The bus stop proved to be an educational place. I studied people standing waiting for the bus. They all seemed so unhappy and downtrodden. It seemed that life in the city had beaten them down. I compared them to the people I had left behind in my little country town. The difference was striking. The light seemed to have gone out in most of the faces at the bus stop. They seemed made of stone hardened by life in the city.

I vowed to never let the city take my smile. We used to sing a song that said, "joy is mine and you can't take it." Old people said that was like the challenge of Job in the bible story. When everything was going great for Job he was a good and faithful servant of God. So the dark force said it is because he has not been tested, let me take away his wealth. Well taking away my car was the first strike but I held fast to my smile. The car was tied directly to my wealth and ability to take care of myself financially.

Not having a car slowed me down tremendously. It slowed me down so much that the old rocking chair blues almost got the best of me. I started thinking about this old boyfriend I had. I couldn't get enough of him. As my sister would say, "you could drink his bathwater, couldn't you?"

Whenever things got tough I would crawl back in his bed. That was tough times and I responded as usual. I called him up and the rest was easy. I was back in his arms and for a few hours all was right with the world.

I was still going like a bunny rabbit. Then I lost my apartment because the money I calculated didn't happen like I thought. So I moved in with a friend and her husband. I guess I wasn't the best roommate because her husband hated having me there. He greeted me with scorn each time we met. I started to feel depressed. It was taking me down but I refused to give up my smile.

The dark force said, she still smiles because she still has her health. Take her health away and she will surely give up that smile. That was when I found out that I was pregnant. My boyfriend suggested that I get an abortion. He knew that was out of the question. It should have been a joyous occasion but it wasn't. I needed a place to live and some better transportation.

The clouds parted a little and a ray of sunlight shone on me. I got my own apartment but still no car and very little money. Getting around without a car seemed to get harder and harder. I walked a long distance to the grocery store and got a cab back. I figured that was the best way to save money. I caught the bus an hour away and then walked two miles to pick up a small Ruby Kate Cosmetics order. Then walked back to the bus for another hour ride home. I washed clothes in the tub and hung them on the line, another one of my money saving ideas. I guess you can say, I over did it because I started to have trouble with the pregnancy.

I ended up in the hospital alone having a baby at six months of the pregnancy. That was not the way to find out that you were number nine on a list of one to ten (one being the top) in the relationship with the father of the child. One nurse let me see the baby before it died. I sank really low. Then another nurse asked the hospital minister to come in to talk with me. She felt like I was suicidal. I didn't think I was suicidal but I knew I was all alone.

I went back to my apartment and recuperated. I guess the calculator was packed away somewhere. I was no longer adding and subtracting the latest money making scheme. I was slowly joining the ranks of the city dwellers, scratching out a living with little to no resources.

Something wasn't right. I was feeling sick. So I went to the hospital Emergency Room. The Emergency Room is what poor people use as the doctor visit. Thirty to seventy people could be crammed into that room at any given time. So I just crammed myself into the room with the rest of my people.

My name was finally called after several hours. The doctor said that they had left the packing inside me after the still birth. He said I had an infection because of it. That sounded like crazy talk. Why, how, what! The doctor removed the packing and gave me a large shot in my buttocks. I couldn't wait to get out of there.

The dark force had almost blocked out the light. I was not smiling. I was devastated. I had lost my car, my apartment, and my health. I was so frail that one more test might have taken me all the way down.

As I made my way through the revolving door, a good looking young man spoke to me. I managed a smile. I couldn't believe it. I smiled. I smiled even though everything had been stripped from me. I still had my smile. That was the beginning of pulling myself up. The city had not won. The dark force had not won. It had not beaten me down. I realized that as long as I could smile, then I could take a big leap over the stress of city living.

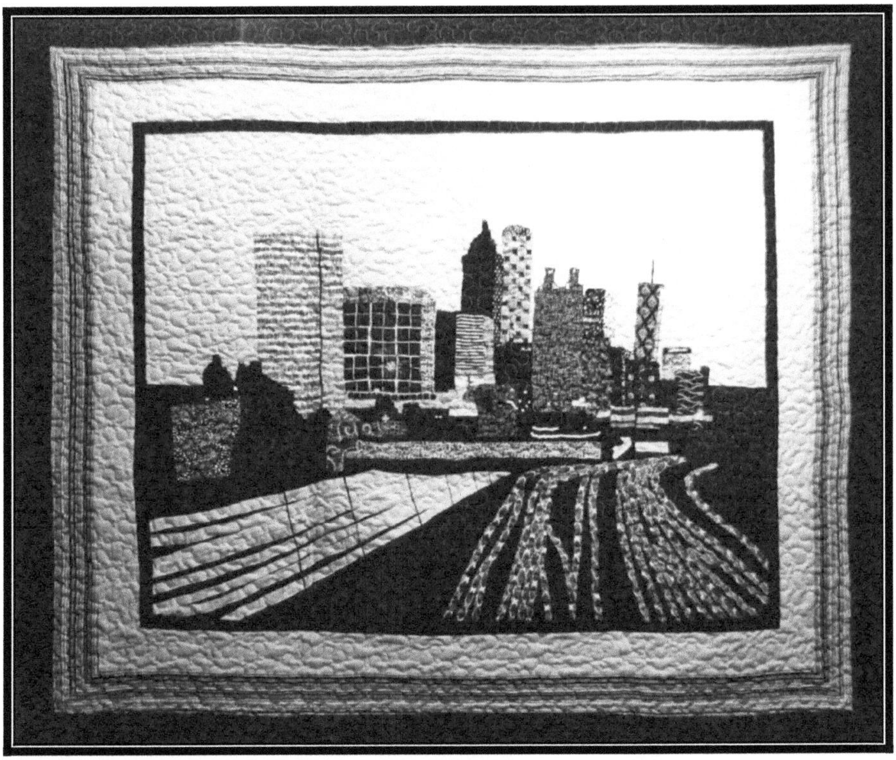

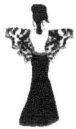

A-T-L
The Atlanta Skyline in black and white. This quilt was
made in 2009 and was the springboard for my journey
into art quilts.

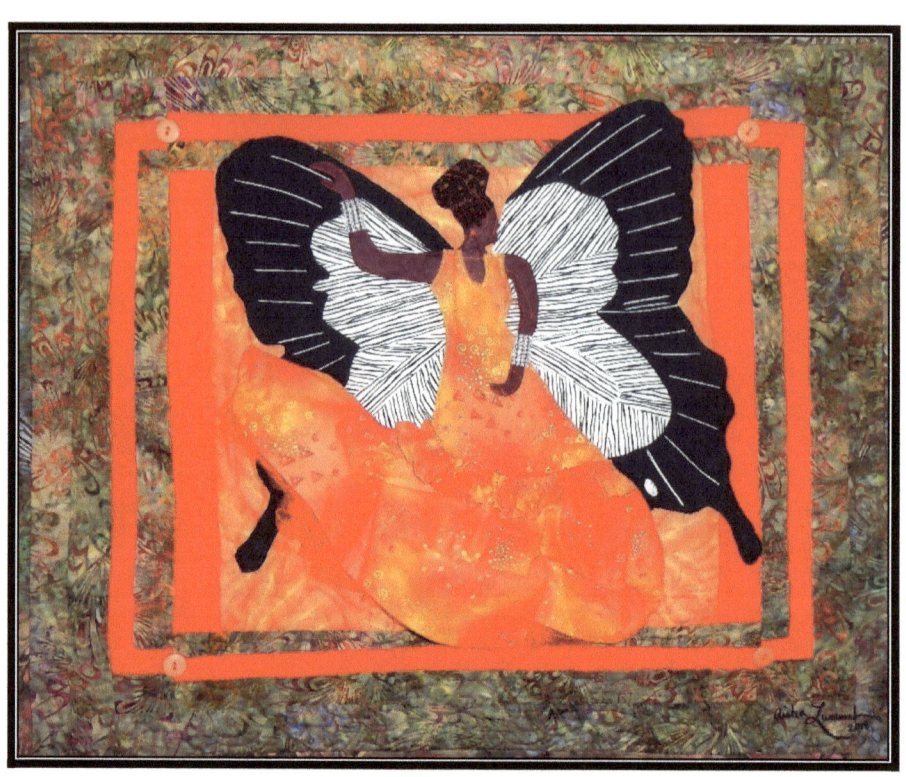

11
LOVE TO DANCE

"You may never dance again," the doctor said. I looked at him suspiciously. He said, "you will have a hard enough time learning to walk again. It is going to take months, maybe years of therapy."

My sister rushed into the room. She shook me and said, "you were screaming again." Sure I was. I was reliving the accident. I could see the blinding light heading straight for us. I was screaming my head off. Then the lights went out.

I slept until the lights came back on. When I woke up I

was in the hospital with family members all around. They were so surprised and happy to see me.

Melanie ran to the door and yelled, "Doctor, Doctor, Nurse she's awake. They all ran to the bed and started hugging me. I could hardly move. I was in some kind of traction. My mom, Cousin Betty, my sister Melanie and Uncle John were there. Uncle John smelled like Irish Spring soap and Cousin Betty was the town crier. I think people actually hired her to cry at funerals. She could really wail.

Uncle John always wore something green. He must have 30 different green shirts. I asked him one day why he wore green so much. He said, "it is the luck of the Irish." His "azz" wasn't Irish. He must be sniffing that soap. I laughed and so did he.

How long have I been here?, I asked. "About three months," Uncle John said. "We have been taking turns waiting on you to wake up."

My eyes searched the room and met my mom's eyes. I looked at mom and I knew. She dropped her head and I said, go on. Tell me, what happened to Joe. The room got extremely quiet. "Joe didn't make it," Melanie said. In that instance, I wanted to die too.

I just keep reliving that over and over and over. I relived the moment that the doctor leaned over me and said that I had a spinal injury. " You will need physical therapy. Rehabilitation will help you regain strength in your limbs. You will start in a wheelchair and eventually you may be able to walk again, but you probably may never dance," explained the doctor.

Never dance. Never dance. Never dance. That echoed in my head and made no sense. I had to dance again. I lived to dance. I loved to dance.

The rehabilitation was hard. The therapist was a big strong Amazon looking woman. I tried to cry about the routine. Mrs. Moreno didn't play. She was one of those children that stayed inside during recess. "It's going to hurt but you have to push past the pain," she would say. "Push past the pain." Really now.

The more Ms. Moreno said, "push past." The more I pushed. I eventually got out of the wheel chair. I stopped hating her that day. She kept working with me and I cried less and less. Months flew by, then I walked with a cane. Dancing again was in the back of my mind. I listened to music religiously and danced in my imagination. I was never giving up on dancing.

Two years of hard times with Mrs. Moreno and I was walking. I saw her smile for the first time when I walked alone. My coordination was still off but I was walking. Each day I got stronger and stronger.

Melanie was about tired of me living with her even though the nightmares and screams had subsided. I knew it wouldn't be long before I could go back to my own home.

I sat on the porch listening to the birds sing. I saw Joe walk up the walkway. He disappeared as he got close to me. I closed my eyes and took a deep breath. Tears rolled down my face. I sat there for a while crying. Then I heard music. It was our favorite dance song on the radio.

I got up from my pity party and turned the music up loud. I danced around and smiled. I was not smooth but I was dancing. I was dancing. I loved to dance.

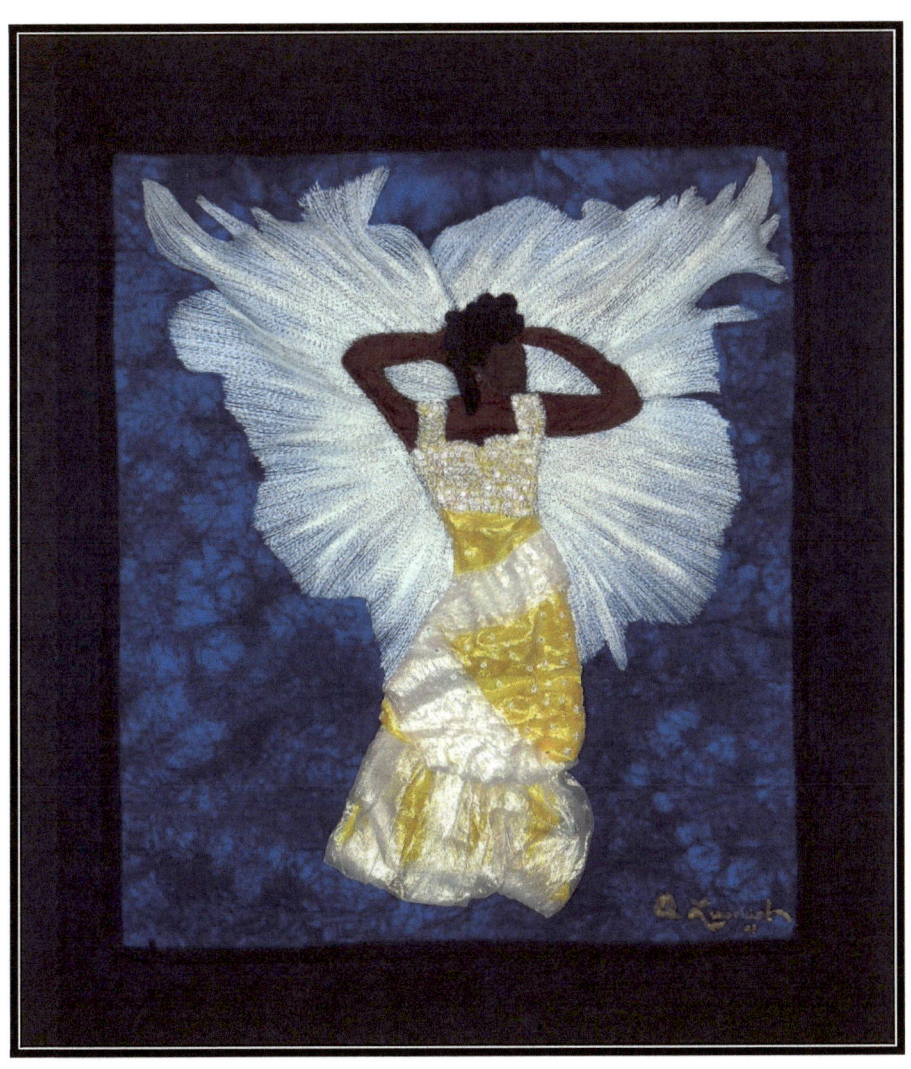

12
ONLY WOMEN HAVE WINGS

I thought for the longest time that I would never find and keep a love. I was truly blessed with two great loves in my life.

I was a happy little girl until it happened to me. It was

my aunt's husband. The way he looked at it, I was not his blood kin. I was only nine years old and he put the light out in me. I became the quiet one that nobody noticed.

I finally told my mother about what had happened to me. She stroked my face and said, "oh my." She sat down and patted the bed for me to sit beside her. Then her arms stretched around me. She said in a whisper, "I am so sorry that happened to you but I am going to tell you a secret. Only women have wings." I looked up at her to see if she was kidding. Her eyes seemed differently truthful. I asked if it was just a story she was making up to make me feel better. "No," she said, "that is why men try to steal that magic away from us."

"You will see that late at night when everybody is asleep, you will be able to untuck your wings and fly around. You'll see," mother told me with a firmness in her voice.

I got married at seventeen to Ralph. I was happy to start my own life. I was happy to be in a place with a man that would protect me. We were able to move into a little house that he bought with his army savings. He was a hard worker and turned out to be a really good father.

It seemed like I was constantly pregnant. We had four stair steps before we knew it and were expecting one more. That one baby turned into two. Ralph was overjoyed about the twins. I was happy too and enjoying this new life with less strife.

The twins were girls which made us have four girls and two boys. By the time the twins were about three years old Ralph started to complain about feeling tired all the time. He never complained about anything. I was a little worried. I urged him to go to the doctor but he was hesitant.

Finally, he promised to go on Friday. He didn't wake up that Thursday morning. I was devastated. I didn't know how to take care of any business. And what would I do with six children alone.

Over in the night I woke up and felt something jutting out from under my shoulder blades. I tugged at it and my wings unfolded. Tears streamed down my face as I remembered my mother's strange story. I took them out for a spin. She was right. It was wonderful to rise about all the pain and uncertainty. I woke up and looked around hoping to see evidence that I was really flying and not dreaming but only the wonderful feeling was still with me.

I gave up the house after struggling for a year to take care of the bills. I moved to public housing. The children were happy there because the streets were filled with children of all ages. It was a diverse community with young families sprinkled with senior citizens here and there. The elders helped guide the children.

Carrie and her family moved in about the same time as we did. She and her husband had the same set of stair steps that I did. They had more boys than us.

We became fast friends and I learned quickly that she liked to party. She introduced me to a night scene that I never knew existed. I could count on her to say be ready at eight on Friday night. I wondered if Carrie had wings as well but I didn't dare ask because if she did that would mean she had something real painful that she probably did not want to share. So I just enjoyed our friendship and flew around at night whenever I needed relief.

We would go to the American Legion, where the Friday

night party was happening. Everybody knew Carrie. When we walked in, people started clamoring for her attention. She acknowledged each and every one.

It was a juke joint, no band and sometimes a DJ, plenty of drinks and food. Not just any food—Soul food. I wasn't much of a dancer but I was real good at holding the table I found that my wings were not needed so much. I slept through the night without flying escapades.

I saw a long tall drink of sweet tea walk across the room. He stopped at our table and said, "My name is Larry and I have been watching you," he confessed. That made me a little nervous. Why was he watching me? "I've been waiting on the right time to introduce myself because a beautiful woman like you should not be sitting alone," he said. I felt my face blushing. I had not given it permission to respond that way but he caught me off guard. "What's your name young lady?" he asked with a sheepish grin that flashed a gold tooth in the dim club light. I hadn't been called a young lady in a long time.

My name is Jeannie, I said. We talked all night. The others came and went from the table to the dance floor. It felt like there was no one else in the room. That is how I met the second love of my life.

"I already know about your children and I just want to tell you that I love children," he said. Do you know that I have six children, I said. "Yes, I know. I told you that I love children," he said with that same grin that always made me smile.

We had some sort of dating. There is not much dating that can happen with six children under foot. After what seemed like forever, but was actually six months. Larry asked me to marry him. I was happy to say yes.

I was married again and happy. Larry turned out to be so loving and attentive. He would sneak up behind me while I was washing dishes, put his hands around my waist and kiss the back of neck. Every woman likes that. He would open doors for me and bring his check home on Friday so we could decide together how the money would be spent.

We were soon adding to our family. The years past by really fast and we worked our way through the downs and thoroughly enjoyed the ups. We loved each other enough to work on it.

They say that time flies when you are having a good time. We were having a good time and the time flew by. Our children were graduating from high school and moving out fast as a cheetah chasing a gazelle. Soon we were home all alone.

People were calling to ask how I liked the empty nest. Well I loved it, but couldn't sound too enthusiast because everybody else was sad to see their children leave home. I was not.

Larry and I sat on the porch and watched the sunset. We watched a little TV, worked word search puzzles, talked about everything under the sun and laughed a lot.

As they say, we lived happily ever after the children grew up and I had my wings for whenever I needed them.

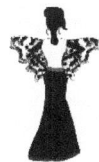

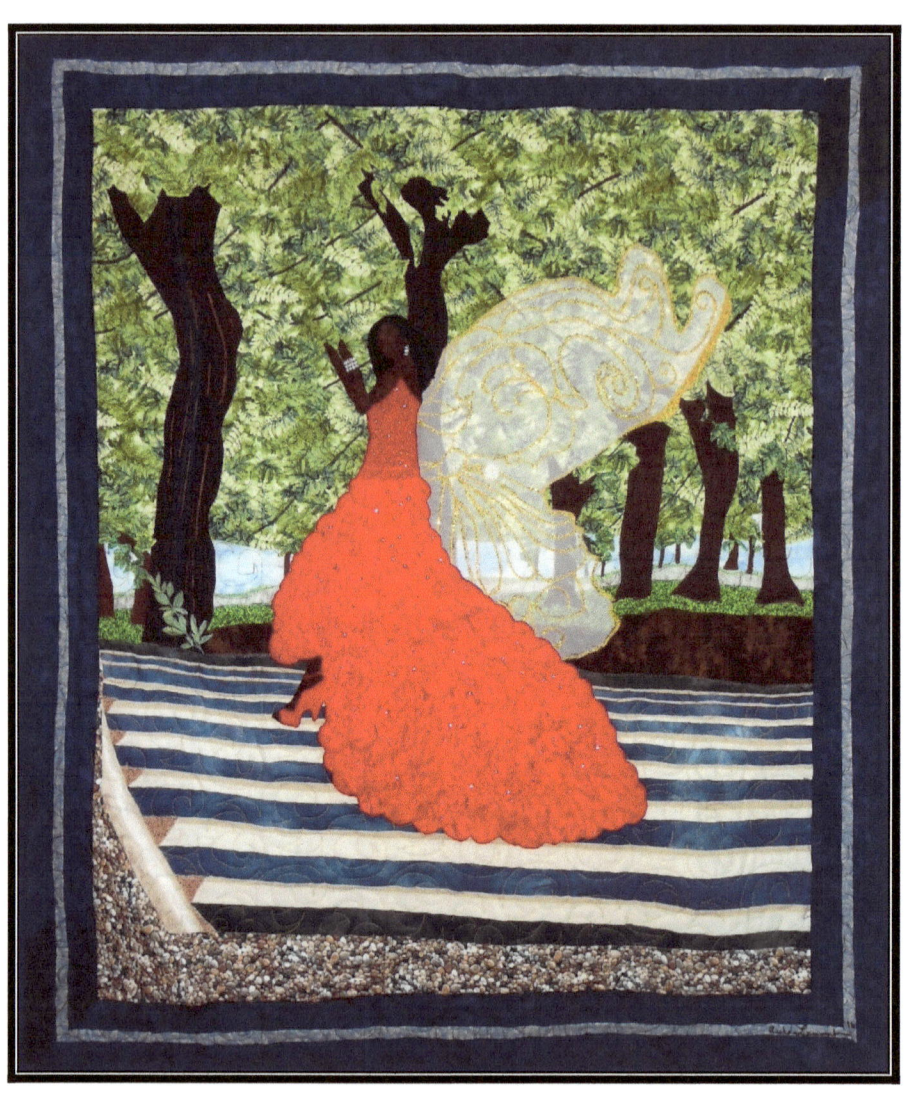

13
PARTY IN THE PARK

My favorite Ray Charles song is "What'd I say." When I was a little girl my grandmother loved to listen to Ray Charles. We would dance all around her kitchen as the music played and she prepared food. I often imagined that

I would be "the girl with the RED DRESS on." The twist was the only dance I really knew how to do because my Granny showed me how to do it.

I loved spending time with Granny and listening to her stories. She told me stories of getting up really early in the morning to make biscuits or pancakes for the family. "I would make two dozen biscuits or pancakes from scratch," she would say. Granny had to cook for nine brothers and sisters plus her mom and dad. Sometimes she would slip and say a curse word while telling me a story. Then she would say, "oops my mouth don't know no Sundays." I can see her now grating cabbage for coleslaw while I danced all the way around the table just past her. She would turn and shake her shoulders with cabbage dripping from her hands.

At that very moment I thought I would have Granny forever. I lost her a few years later and my journey to the depths of my being began. I crawled inside myself and shut down.

My previous job supervisor once said that my insolence shows that I must have missed a few whippings when I was young. Of course I beg to differ with that analysis. I think I missed some hugs when I was young. As a matter of fact I remember getting very few hugs when I was young which made me crave affection. I quickly learned to stuff that feeling inside. I became shy and withdrawn. I was good at getting really quiet and shrinking into the background.

One of the male teachers used to hug the older girls. He would throw his arm across their shoulders as they walked down the hall. I didn't understand that nor did I want hugs from a teacher. Teachers to me were very stern, indifferent and aloof. They didn't fit into the image of people that I needed or wanted to give me hugs. Then I started seeing a couple of those older girls go into the closet with one of the male teachers. I had no understanding of that but I could tell from the way other children whispered about it that it was not a good thing. Later in my life, I gave thanks to God that I was not hugged by that teacher.

Eventually a boy showed interest in me. I was able to get unlimited hugs from him. Something unfolded in me when I got those hugs. It was a new feeling that relaxed my inner tension. It was a very new feeling. The grown-ups said I was "fast." I didn't know what fast meant nor did I think I was fast. I felt ignored and overlooked but certainly not fast. Fast didn't last too long before I was hurt again. That is when I put on a suit of armor that helped me navigate the world. Behind my shield I was fragile and broken. I put on an outwardly bold demeanor which was often perceived as insolence.

I had several jobs that didn't suit me. I did my work above and beyond but the managers always seemed to want more.

It was about 6:00 in a Tuesday morning. I walked into the restaurant kitchen and started to set up the food prep for the day. Ms. Becker came in at about 6:15. She looked all around and I knew that meant she was after something to complain about. Boy was she a complainer. "I noticed a spot on the counter and Natalie did not prepare enough eating utensils for the day," she admonished. I jumped in to say how busy we were right up to the closing hour. She pitched in to help with the onslaught, I said. "That is no excuse for her not finishing her work. You obviously are having trouble handling your managing responsibilities. Plus several other things were left unfinished," she said as she looked up at me with glaring eyes. She finished it with her hands on her hips. Whoosh! I caught fire before I knew it. I snapped.

I told Ms. Becker that "I was LOOKING when I found this job." I threw the keys at her and walked out. I surprised myself. I can usually catch that temper before it is unleashed on anyone. It had just piled up too high and I couldn't take anymore.

My life was a constant rotation of jobs and men. My heart was unprepared for all the suitors that would love me and leave me. I was up one day and down in the dumps the next.

I tried to find myself in the eyes of others until that day when I took a long look in the mirror. For the first time I saw my own light in my own eyes. I know that sounds so easy but it wasn't that easy.

It started with the new lady on my job with a gleam in her eyes and a song in her heart. I asked her how did she maintain happiness and joy all the time. She said, "I have a song that I sing to myself each time I am confronted with a difficult situation". She invited me to yoga and meditation classes. I practiced on my own between classes. The change was slow but consistent. Well it was as consistent as my practice. The more I practiced, the better.

Joy came to me. It happened. I was able to will my own joy and the sparkle never left my eyes. I unfolded from within and never looked back. Calm became my constant side-kick which in turn made others want to be my friend.

My new job had a formal party in the park. I couldn't imagine getting all dressed up to go to the park. All my co-workers were talking excitedly about it. This was the fifth year that the party had happened and in the past it was a gigantic success, so said the co-workers. So on Saturday I went to a party in the park.

When I reached the top of the steps I shouted, "Wu hoooooo Party over here." And all my friends rushed over and gave me a big hug.

The Process

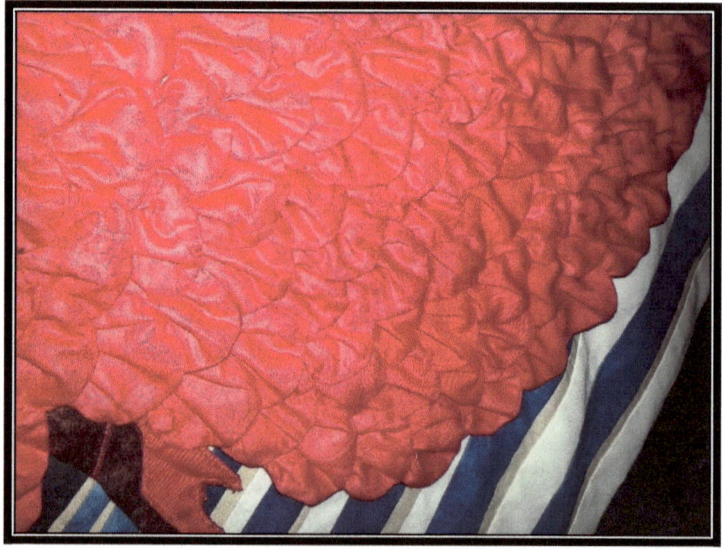

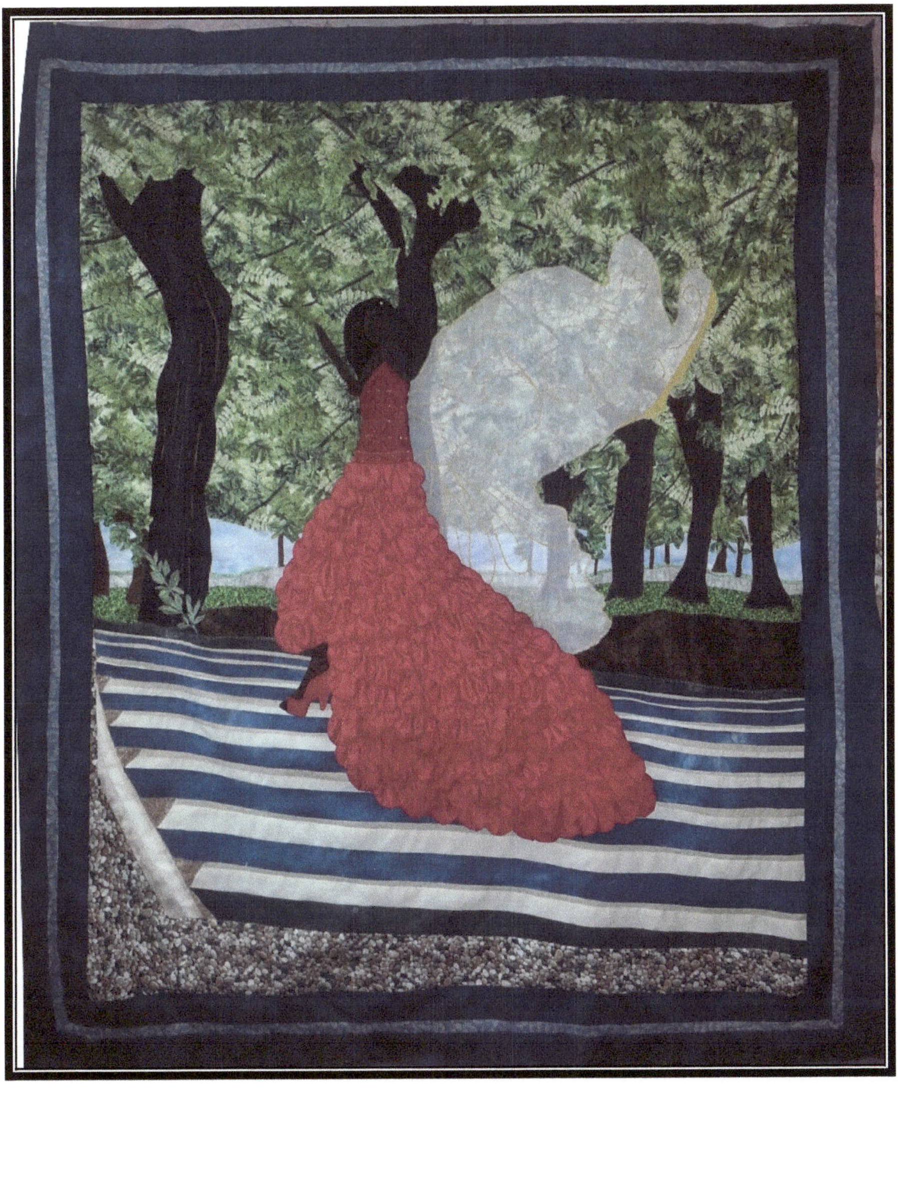

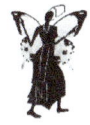

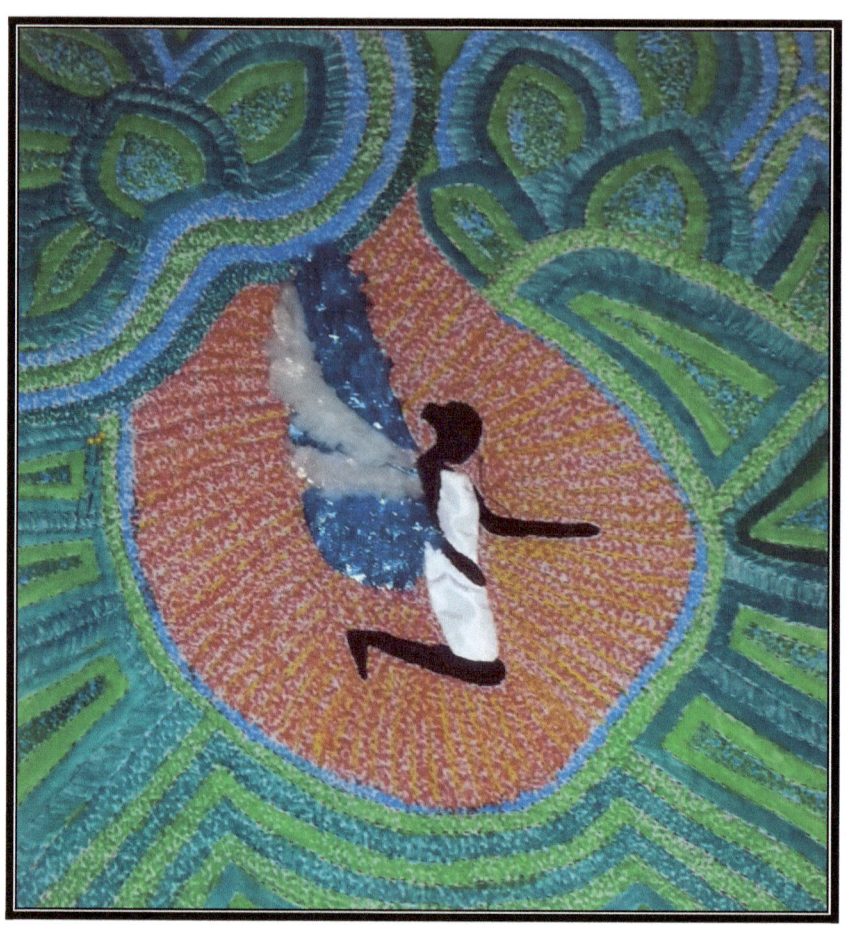

14
PAT'S PRAYER

The color was finally slipping back into my life. I was able to laugh again and even dance. I felt as though I had come back from a long trip. Now I'm getting ahead of myself. Let me start at the beginning of this story.

My oldest child died. He was just old enough to take a hold of his world. He had plans. I was not ready for him to leave. The day it happened I felt as though I fell down a deep dark hole. I was so numb that I didn't even care to climb out. I just let myself tumble, sink and fall deeper and deeper. I went through the motions daily of work but I shut down the part of my being that governed feelings. I couldn't stand to feel because it hurt too much.

My two daughters tried to reach me but I was unreachable. I was torn between wanting to be reached and not wanting to be reached. I could see the pain on their faces but I couldn't do anything to make it better. My own pain had a grip on me that felt like I was covered in a cloak of heavy fog that would not allow me to move.

People would give me their condolences with all manner of kind words. I smiled and even gave hugs but they could tell I was not there. In my mind, I was sitting somewhere in a dark cave praying that my son would come back to me.

I stayed in there as long as I could. Then one day a little light interrupted my darkness. I was suspicious of it. How did it get in?, I thought. This was my sacred dark place, but it just kept shining through the darkness. I wanted it to go away but it wouldn't. It kept shining there and I kept ignoring it.

It was shining so bright that I couldn't ignore it any longer. I walked over to the light. It made me feel a little something. I felt a little something that I had not felt in a long time. Shortly after I accepted it, I started to see a little color. The light grew and more colors started to come in.

I was so weak that all I could do was look at the light and the colors. I was not ready to let it come inside of me yet. I kept an eye on it as it grew day by day. Then one day I smiled. My youngest daughter caught me smiling. She couldn't believe it. She made a little joke about my smile being crooked but she was still happy to see it. I felt a twinge of energy that I associated with the light.

Color would no longer be denied. Green swirled around me. It almost danced on my heels. Blue followed close behind it and poked its head in and out of the green. Days turned into months and colors slowly entered my world.

Red marched in boldly and announced that it would surround me with warm loving feelings. I know I had smiled once but I am not sure if I was ready to receive warm loving feelings or give warm loving feelings. Orange slipped in and fanned all around the red. I caught myself enjoying the show of colors.

I looked around for purple. I was waiting on purple to make an entrance. Purple used to be my favorite color when I had joy in my heart. I bathed in the light of the colors and enjoyed them. I breathed in slow and deep and felt the green come into my being and heal some damaged parts. Blue, green, red and orange danced around, but still no purple. The hardened shell loosened from around my body. I knew I would have to come out before too long.

My husband was so patient with me as I went through my search for the answers of life. I wanted to know why some people are taken away and others allowed to stay a long long time. He was suffering from the same loss but it seemed that his faith was unshakeable. I thought mine was too until the earth moved beneath my feet and I fell.

Now I am standing up again. My legs are a little wobbly but I am standing again. I am less and less tempted to go back to that dark place. I still miss my baby but the realization that he is not coming back is getting real. So I search for new ways to honor him. I find new ways to celebrate his life. I find strength in knowing that he was here and I held him in my arms when he was just a toddler.

I found my strength in Faith. For the longest time it was hard to find my center. Faith felt so distant. As soon as I renewed my faith, I saw a tiny sliver of purple hoovering in the corner of my awareness. Joy filled my heart and I realized that I had to let my light shine for both my son and myself.

I started giving big hugs to everyone and even smiling. My church family was amazed at my new energy. I was alive again and happy. What can I say? Some of us have to go up the rough side of the mountain. It was a really hard lesson but I got it.

The Process starting with white whole cloth.

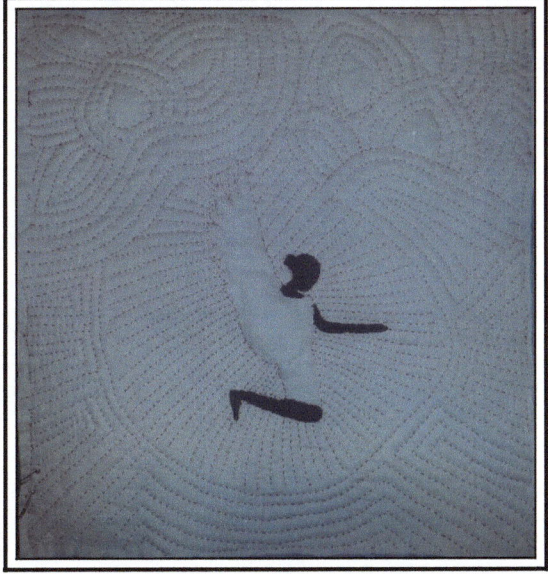

Aisha Lumumba

The Process

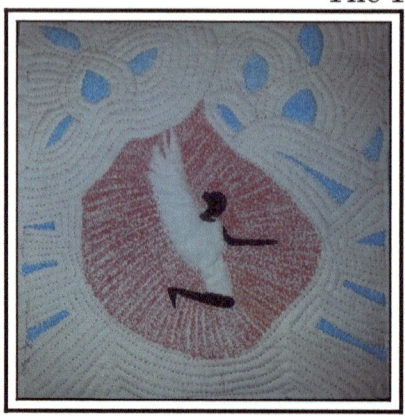 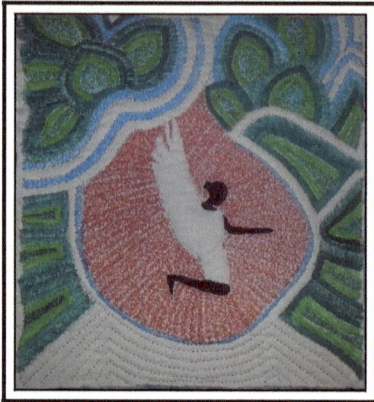

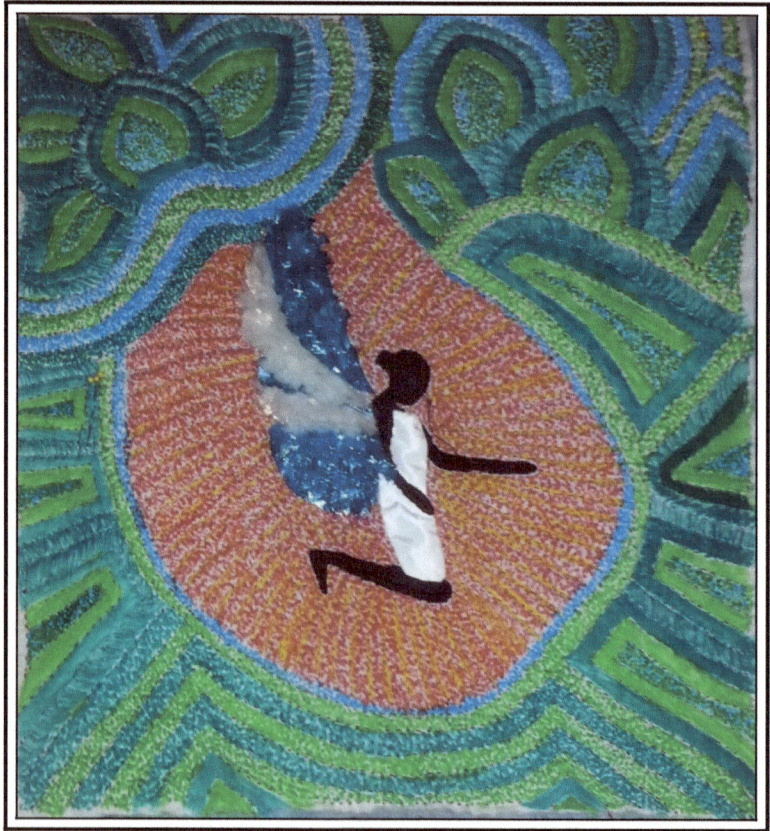

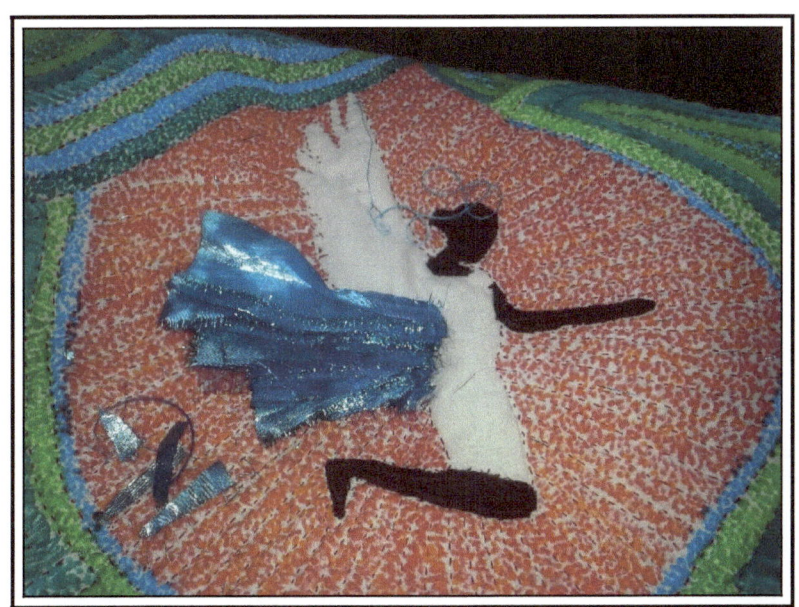

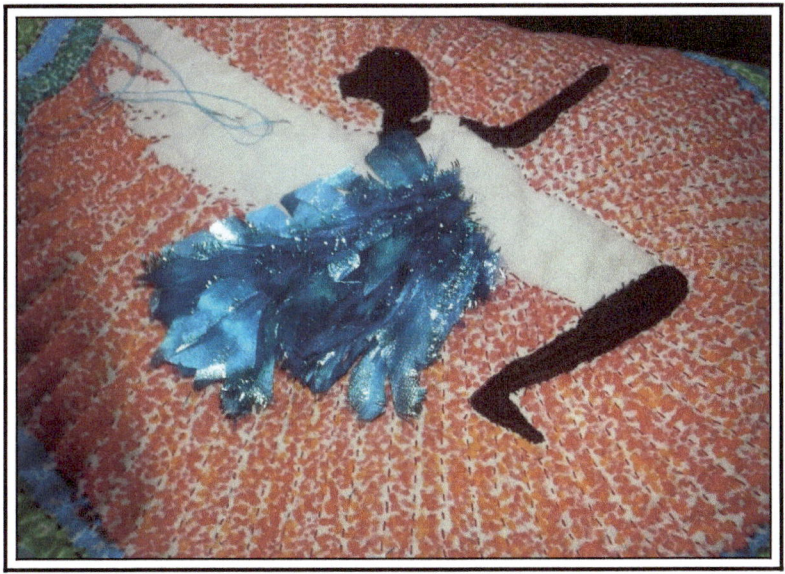

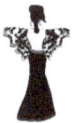

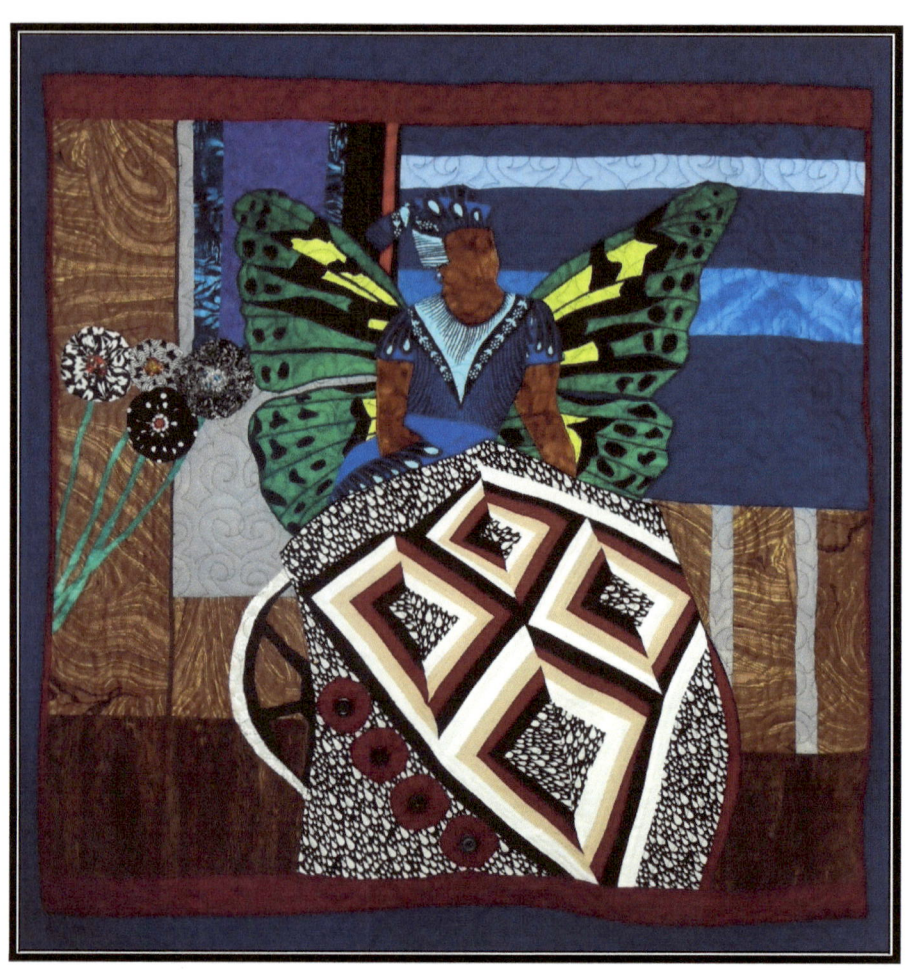

15
QUILTERS CAN FLY

I grew up in a family of hard workers, so I followed suit. My mother, my father and my grandmother were all fabric lovers. My mother and father were tailors while at the same time my grandmother was a quilter. Her projects seemed to take a lot longer to make but were so welcomed and needed.

Our parents set the bar for time management. My sisters watched and learned. As a young girl I watched my sisters work really hard. They were always doing something. So I worked hard as well. I thought everyone in the world worked hard like we did. I think I was in the 6th grade before I realized that other people did not have that same work ethic.

I was introduced to sewing early in my life. My grandmama reeled me in and taught me to sew by hand. She used to make yoyos all the time. One day she pushed her glasses back on her nose and said, "come here little fast girl and let me show you how to make yoyos." At that time, I didn't think it was anything that I wanted to do, but we couldn't talk back to our elders. I couldn't even let on that I was thinking adverse thoughts. We were led to believe that lightning would strike us down if we talked back to our elders. And if you didn't believe that, you knew for sure that mom or dad would knock hell out of you.

I loved quilting with my grandmother but in my teenage years it was too slow for me. I learned how to make clothes and the speed of the sewing machine was all I wanted. I was a happy teenager because I could whip up a skirt or a new outfit in no time. It was a good thing that I could sew clothes, otherwise I would not have had the latest fashions. Every now and then Grandmama would catch me as I tried to tip past her. "Come here and make some yoyos," she said. Making the yoyos would slow me down for a while and that was her goal.

When prom time came, I already knew what I was going to wear. I saw a dress in a magazine that I had to have. Lucky for me I had the skills to make that dress. I made the waist a little lower so I would look taller. Then I cut it so that it would accentuate my thighs. The dress was the envy of all who attended; and I guess I was the envy too since I was inside the dress. I was so happy that I had that skill.

Life was really sweet to me. I married fairly young and had three beautiful children. We travelled and lived in several different places. Traveling gave me the opportunity to learn a lot of new and different things. I became an artist as I dabbled into different crafts and art disciplines. My involvement in the arts took me back to quilting beside my grandmother. I had never thought of what she did as art. I started to see the quilting lessons in other art forms.

I saw Grandmama's patterns in stain glass and in hook rugs. I painted and could hear her explaining color theory. I didn't know it was color theory. I just thought she knew what colors looked good together. My grandmother would put shapes together and make a new shape. I learned later that she was using shapes to give her art dimension. I thought she was just throwing pieces of scraps together only to understand later in my life that she used abstract and implied art principles. Now she didn't call it that but her work was creatively awesome.

One day tragedy struck and I found myself in the hospital paralyzed. My world turned upside down in an instant. I let a bad attitude attach itself to me. I thought my life was over, although I had survived the accident. I couldn't see how I would go forward. I was differently abled. It was daunting. Someone told me that I was paraplegic and would be confined to a wheelchair. At first that sounded so finite.

I went through the therapy and witnessed great support from my family. My family taught me that I had to stop feeling sorry for myself. They said I had to get up and make something of my life. So I eventually did. I remembered what Grandmama told me. She would lean back in her rocking chair and say, "you can't get ready for the big day, you have to BE ready." I started making yoyos for my quilts and learning to take care of myself. The more I quilted the better I felt. I found myself and my strength in the creative process.

My love for quilting stands out in the midst of my peers. I don't think it is because I have any special powers. I attribute my quilting skills to the fact that I work harder than any of my peers. I get in a groove and I eat, sleep, and drink quilting. I study the process. I try new things. I dream about quilting. I make my own fabric and create some fantastic results.

Nowadays I put yoyos on most of my quilts. I give thanks for such a loving grandmama who still gives me inspiration long after she has gone.

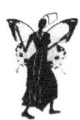

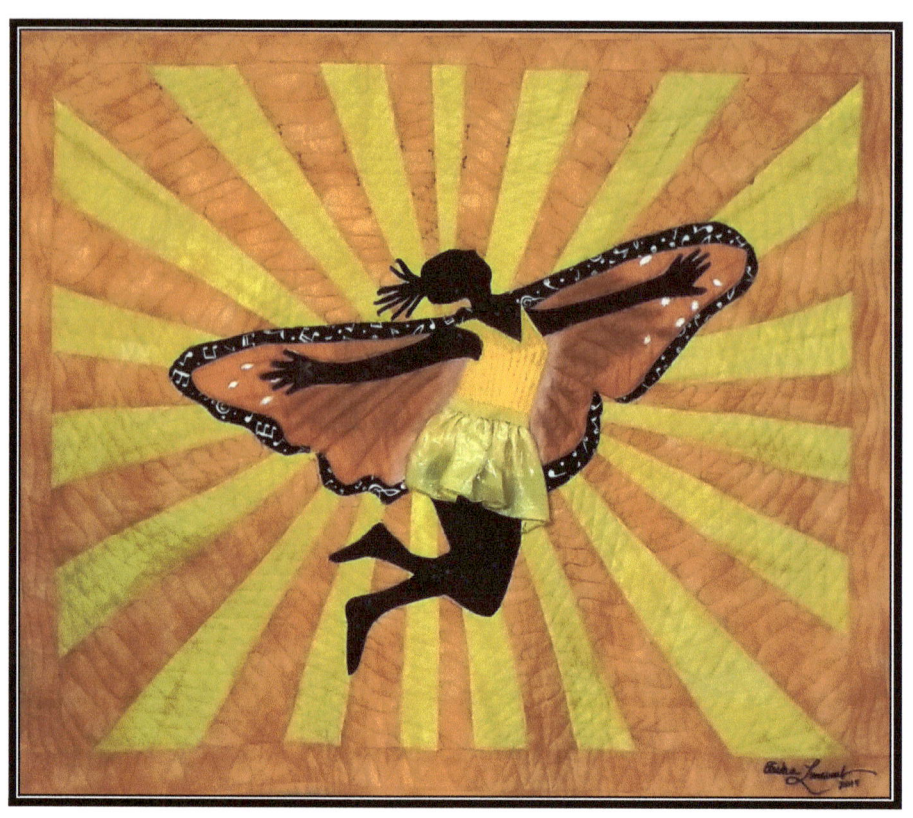

16
SOAR

It's Christmas and I have to see my damn Dad again. I thought he would be dead by now, since he is struggling with a deadly illness, but he's not. He is still limping around expecting somebody to forgive him. I don't know if I am the forgiving one. I don't know if I am ready yet.

Friends tell me that I have to let go and forgive. One lady told me that forgiving does not mean forgetting. She said that as long as I hold on to the hatred that I am holding my own heart hostage. I am not sure that I understand any of that or know what it will mean for my future.

When I see him, I am instantly transported back in time. I am transported to a really miserable time when I could hardly breathe because I was hiding in a cramped space. I am transported to a time when I got my nerve up to say no only to be mentally punished.

Dad would tell me that if I did not comply he would beat my mother. When she came in from work, he would start an argument that would eventually end in a beating. I laid in my bed and listened to her screams. I felt so bad. I had to save her because I thought he might kill her and I thought I could save her. God forbid he killed her and we were left with him.

As a child I thought that I had to keep her safe from his violent temper, so I stopped saying no. I resorted to hiding, but I could only hide so long. The old people said he was damaged goods and that my mother never should have married him. I got the worst of it.

The day I met my teacher, Miss Grimes was the most blessed day of my life. She was a petite little lady with big puffy hair. The hair style made her look taller than us children. She saw something in me. Miss Grimes noticed that I did not look people in the eye, that I was quietly withdrawn, and internally troubled. She gave me books, wonderful books.

I gobbled up the words in the books like a black widow spider on her spouse. I travelled the world and beyond riding on the wings of the words. My family called me the family-book-worm. I loved it. Finally, I was something other than my dad's whipping board. I was a proud book-worm.

The Christmas tree was in the window and the sound of

Christmas carols was booming from the house. My knees knocked but I knew I had nothing to fear. I felt that fear choking me right in the center of my throat. I hadn't been home in so long. I wouldn't be here now if my mother had not begged me to come. She said that Dad was dying and it would be our last Christmas together. I don't know if I came to see him dead once and for all or if I wanted my mother to be happy having us all home.

Mom opened the door and I dove into her arms. I jumped at that hug before I knew it. She was not usually a hugger. She gave back a halfhearted hug. It didn't take me long to come to my senses and remember where I was. I let go slowly.

I was someone else in my new life. I was loved by my friends and family. I had forgotten this terrible place with its cold glaring accusatory walls staring at me. I forgot that we didn't exchange hugs or show any other sign of caring. That probably followed us here from slavery times, when we didn't dare show caring for fear that the one we cared for would be sold away as some sort of punishment. We probably guarded our hearts by not letting ourselves love too deeply because the loved one could be taken away in an instant, either by being sold or death.

All the skills I had learned in counseling and therapy had to come forth and save me now. Before the therapy, I wore the shame on my sleeve. I thought I was the evil one, the bad one. As a young child I thought I had caused the problem. Now I know better and I am in a constant struggle to make my feelings match my knowledge.

Aunt Linda rushed past me and pushed me inside the door as she went by. Her wig was on sideways as usual. I don't think she paid my hesitation any attention. She was always in a stumbling hurry. She knew a drink of something strong had her name on it.

The house was filled with family. Everybody had staked out a place to sit. It was like musical chairs, if you got up you might lose your seat. Cousin Liz would be asking anyone that walked by to get her a refill. I chuckled as I remembered being the child to run for refills.

The men had gathered outside. They usually hid a bottle under the chair and a cup somewhere nearby. The ones that could still smoke puffed away while the ones that were not supposed to enjoyed and inhaled deeply. They talked incessantly, laughed hardy and, as the women said, they told a lot of lies.

The smell of good food wafted through the house. I was already breathing slowly and deeply to arrest my stress. So a new and pleasant smell entered my nose with each sniff. Oh boy, mom made my favorite sweet potato pies.

I stopped at the dining room and looked around. So far so good. My mom caught my wondering eyes. She nodded her head towards the bedroom and said, your dad will get up when it is time to eat. Good, I thought. That will give me more time to prepare. I had kept that secret far too long.

My counselor helped me give the secret up. She explained to me that as long as I kept the secret, I gave him power over me. Today will be the last step towards my healing. I found a seat in a corner and settled in while laughing at the family jokes. Cousin April always told the funniest stories unless her brother Jacob was around. We thought that they must practice making jokes at home.

Mom announced that dinner was ready. People on the couch bounced up, all but Aunt Linda. She rocked back and forth a couple of times trying to get up.

Someone seated beside her gave her a push. We all got up from our prospective corners and made a big circle. My dad came in leaning on a cane. He looked nothing like the man I knew. He was so thin and crippled. He was a sad shell of a man with no hair and withering limbs. I wanted to feel sorry for him but I couldn't.

I really looked at him. I didn't turn away with fear. I didn't have to drop my head in shame. I was able to face it all down. The man in that chair was no longer the overpowering tiger that took advantage of a frail and frightened little child. He was pitiful. There were plenty of people in the family that pitied him. Pity was not what I was feeling.

I checked my feelings to see exactly what was going on with me. All the hours of therapy, meditation, and self-introspection had paid off. I wasn't feeling anything. I was really free. By that time, Uncle James finished blessing the food and I could truly say AMEN.

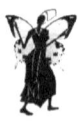

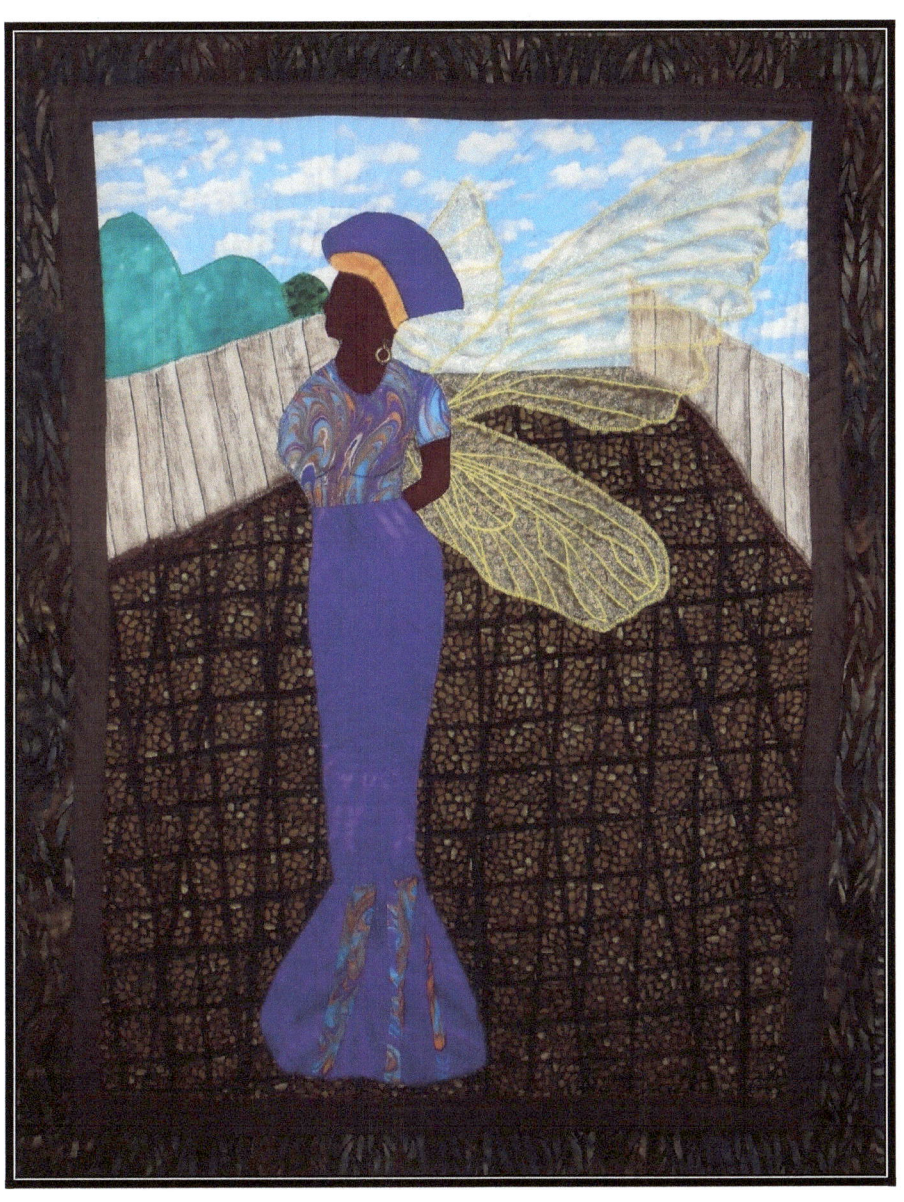

17
STANDING TALL

I stayed when most other women would have left. I knew for a long time but I kept quiet about it. I found that it is real easy to say what you will do when you are not in the situation. It gets a lot harder when you are face to face with it. It is especially hard when you have to weigh the effects it will have on a lot things, including your children. He had a wondering eye that I noticed early in the relationship, before we got married. I thought marriage would change that. He changed for a while. When it started up again, I asked myself what was I supposed to do. He was not physically abusive. We had some really good sweet years. The years passed pretty fast while we worked and built a family.

The google eyes came back slowly. I started to notice that he was giving other women a lot of extra attention. Then he started coming in later from work and saying that he was at happy hour. His job switched him to the nightshift. The shift ended at one a.m. and I could count on him to be home by two. That changed after a few months.

The phone calls started. Something inside of me knew he was messing around but I wanted to fool myself. I wanted it to go away. It didn't. As a matter of fact, it got worse. He was gone all the time. He would rush home before daylight, just in time to give Nicole a ride to school. When I said something to him, he just shrugged his shoulders and said, "you know I am working." I knew he was NOT working all that time, but that was his way of covering his tracks. It was like he had cookie crumbs all over his face and he said, oh no I'm not eating cookies.

When the word got out, all my friends said I was crazy. They told me I should leave him. It was so easy for them to say that from the comfort of their homes over my phone. I was the one in the thick of it. I was the one loosing on both ends. If I left, I stood to lose everything that I had worked so hard to build. My children would suffer as well. If he left, we would both loose a friendship and relationship that we had built over our young lifetime. And still, the children would suffer.

What if I stayed? I wondered if I could withstand the outer pressure and the inner pressure. Could I stand the shame of being called an old fool behind my back? Could I believe anything he said. He promised he would never tip out on me again? But this time was different, he seemed to be consumed with this woman. Could my heart ever get over the hurt I was feeling? Could I ever trust again?" I had a lot to weigh.

I cried and walked the floor. I cried so much that I wondered where my body got all the water. Some nights I blamed myself. He wasn't taking money out of our home so his outside relationship was based purely on something else. I tried to figure out if he was in love with her, maybe that was why he slept at her house almost every night.

I spent a lot of lonely nights counting the four walls while I tried to come to terms with what I was going to do. Then I would cry some more. Some nights the walls were closing in on me and I felt like I was suffocating. Then other nights it seemed like a big hollow shell that would swallow me up and I would disappear forever. Then I would wake up as he crawled in the bed while the sun peeked in the window through a crack in the curtains.

One day I realized that I had done nothing wrong. I was not less of a woman than the other women. It was his problem and not mine. I was not the one trying to prove that I was somebody special. I was not the one going through a mid-life crisis. It was him. He was the one with a hole in his soul.

That was when I decided that I could hold my head high. I could in fact be still and wait. I became someone else and

I think it frightened him. I no longer yelled and screamed at him. I no longer cried for days on end. I was no longer a ghost of my former self. I had a little pep in my step.

It was around that same time that the other woman dumped him. She put him out of her apartment. She, of all people, told him that she had a conscious and she could no longer watch him rush off to meet the family for Thanksgiving dinner. She said she didn't like having to spend Christmas alone while he entertained as the loving and faithful husband. It was over. He came crawling back into my bed. Home by two a.m.

I was still there but my heart was cold as ice. It really was over for us but we put a good face on it. We played the happy couple for as long as we could, although, we both knew that it was just a matter of time. We would either work it out or end it peacefully. Whatever happened, I would be standing tall.

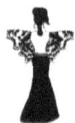

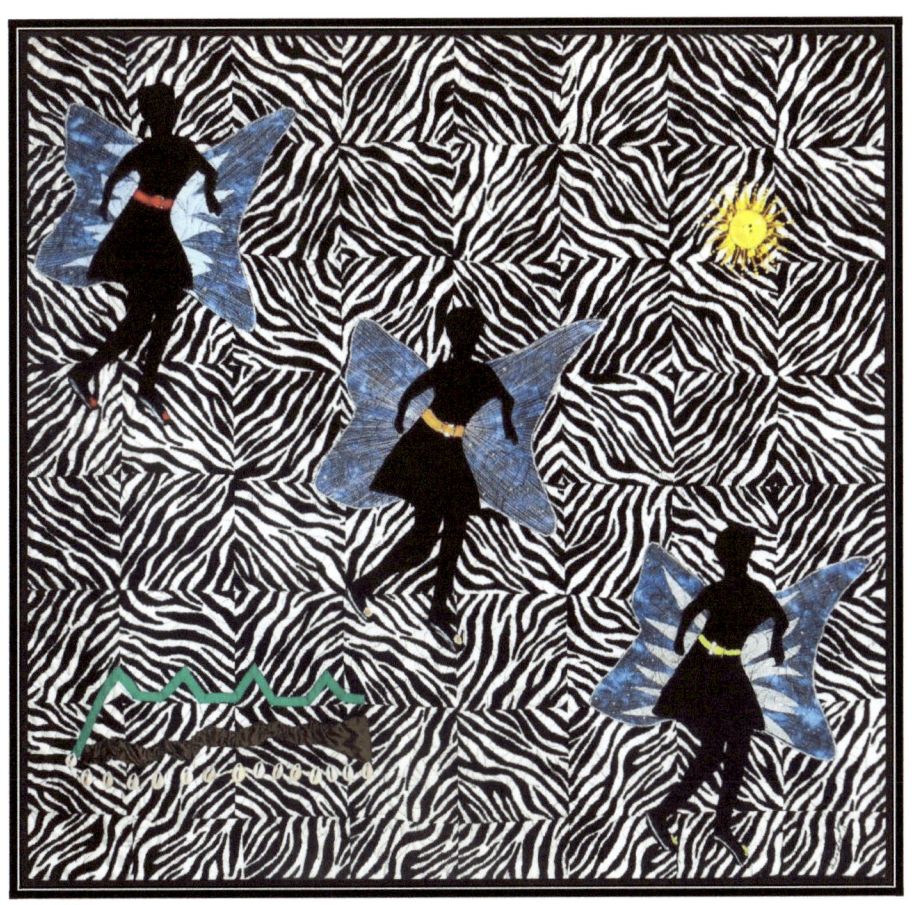

18
THE THREE OF US

I had two really good friends that I loved dearly. We were inseparable. We didn't talk about our friendship as love because that was reserved for relationships with boys and family members.

We were called the ABC Girls. I was Betty, the one suggesting that we stay after school for the basketball game. Amber was cool headed and fun loving at the same time. Carla was no nonsense. Her favorite saying was, "I ain't fooling with ya'll."

We are not going to get you in trouble with your parents, I would say in an attempt to coax her to stay. "Yeah," Amber would chime in, "we already have a ride hooked up." The ride was suspect because about seven or eight of us would pile in the car for the ride as the late fall breeze hummed through the windows.

We were always together. We got in a lot of trouble together. Like the time we got Bobby's uncles' cousin's brother to go to the package store for us. We got high on beer and wine. Helen went home and thought the closet was the bathroom. I am sure her mother cursed us that night.

It was my idea that we all dressed alike for the prom and Amber's idea that we wear our hair alike. Carla chose the shoes. Wish the three of us had taken a picture together but the emphasis was placed on taking a picture with our dates. The dates are all gone from our lives and we are still here.

No one could have ever told us that our friendships would not last the test of time. Time tested us and pulled us far apart. Thirty years passed before we realized how much space had grown between us.

We all went our merry way to create a life for ourselves. We had our children, married some great men and lived our lives apart from each other.

One day I experienced a great upheaval in my life. My husband found someone else to love. I was practically all alone. In my isolation I started to write down my feelings. I was hurting so badly.

They say that hurt people hurt people. I opened my mouth and let some terrible things out of it. I said things that I wish I could take back. I remembered hurting so badly that I just threw mud at every moving target and some that weren't moving. Everybody that got my wrath did not deserve it. The problem was that I couldn't get to the person that I really wanted to hurt so I unwittingly hurt some people who I would need later in my life.

I missed my friends and the old days. I missed them a hell of a lot. It would have been really nice to have them with me on that journey.

We got older and our family and friends started to leave this earth plane. The funerals brought us together again. At one funeral in particular I was so happy to see Amber. I walked over expecting a hug. She held up one finger and said, "just a minute I have to catch Mary Jane." Then she rushed past me to the door. After standing there a while and realizing she wasn't really coming back, I went on to the next thing.

Later I saw Amber across the parking lot talking to some of our high school friends. I decided not to bother her and went on to my car. Amber had been one of those people caught in my misguided mudslinging.

It took me a while to truly believe that she didn't want to be bothered with me but I eventually got the message. And it was understandable. I had wronged her.

Carla on the other hand understood that life dealt each of us a different hand of cards. We each did the best with the hands we had. She also realized better than I, that we would never have those close friendships again.

Carla needed and wanted a resemblance of that

friendship as much as I did. We decided to take a road trip. Left our husbands home and went on a long weekend trip.

Carla still had the ability to like many of the same things that I did and to leave room to dislike as we pleased. I could share with her and never feel judged. She'd just say, "I ain't fooling with you."

Carla still had her good sense of humor. She was straight forward. I never had to guess what she meant. We further renewed our friendship by celebrating our birthdays together. It became an annual tradition. We hoped our husbands would become friends and they did. That made it easier for us to get together more often.

We took the plunge and went on another road trip. We didn't go anywhere associated with work. We went on a real vacation, just the two of us. We went on a Girls- Weekend.

We spent a lot of time in silence as the wheels ate up miles of pavement. We both seemed to need the silence and to enjoy it. Then we started to talk about our lives. We talked about our parents and what we learned growing up. We talked about our siblings. We talked about what it meant to lose our fathers. We talked about our health or the lack of it. We talked about our children and how proud we were of them. We talked about our jobs and other friends we had made along the way. We talked about a lot of things.

Finally on the second day, we talked about ourselves. Growing up had not been easy, especially seeing and accepting our own shortcomings. Life is strange, I said to Carla. You know that time when you and Stanley went to that affair around Thanksgiving time, I said. She nodded and looked down at her trembling hands as if she were remembering something she hoped I would not bring up. Well I always wanted to say how sorry I was that I wasn't with you. I know it was traumatic for you, I whispered. Tears were streaming down her cheeks. The pain was sill raw after all these years. I make an honest attempt to help her through that pain so many years later.

I haven't been able to remember where I was but I am sure I was somewhere thinking only of myself. It was a long time before I learned to care for others. We underestimated how devastating the actions we took in our teen years could have on our lives.

Teenage years were a time of awakening and introduction to our bodies and our inner identity. As I look back, I know that so much was happening so fast. If I could turn back the hands of time, I would change a few things but then I would be interfering with the Divine Plan.

We laughed heartily at the thought that all of what we had been through was a Divine Plan. So all of this was Divine, I said. "I ain't fooling with you girl," Carla said.

We laughed and we cried. Then we prayed together.

We grew ten feet tall that weekend and cemented our friendship forever.

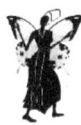

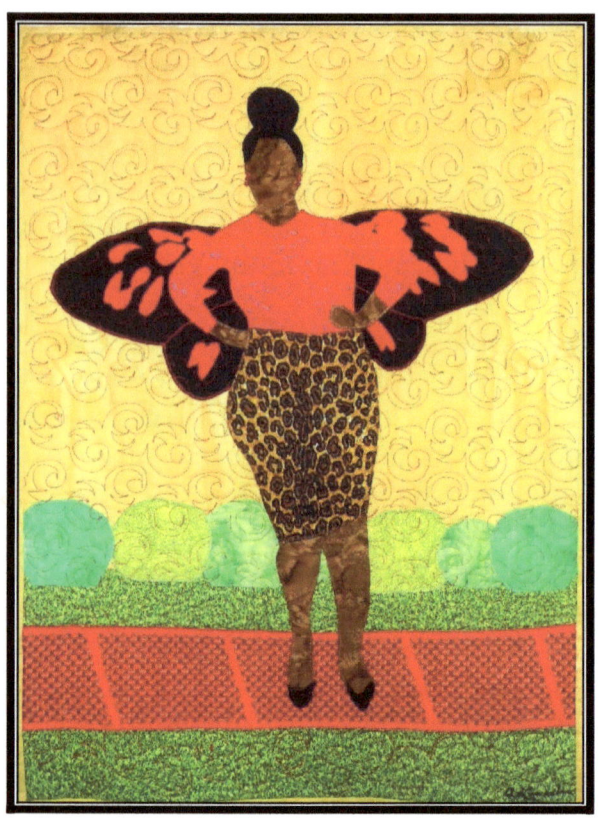

19
WAIT A MINUTE

He left us. He was my husband. The man I made a promise to love and cherish no matter what. That same man that also pledged to love and honor me for the rest of his life. We couldn't find neither love nor honor that day.

That was the worst day of my life. I was so blindsided. He walked in with a dominant air around him. His head held high and shoulders squared like a lion strutting before his pride. I knew that meant trouble. He said, "I'm leaving," as he coolly walked to the room and gathered his things. I stood back and watched. I was broken but didn't let him see it. I couldn't give him the satisfaction.

I stood in the doorway and watched him walk away with as much as he could carry. I wanted to say, wait a minute. His friend Gary was waiting in the car. They drove off slowly. It seemed like the two minutes it took for them to pull out of the parking space lasted an hour. Everything was happening in slow motion.

I was too stunned to cry or too angry to let the cloud burst. This slipped up on me like a thief in the night. I wondered if I would feel better if I had seen some signs. My father used to always say that hindsight is 20/20. I didn't know what that meant for the longest times. Hindsight is kicking in right now. I'm looking back over my marriage and I can see clearly.

We used to go everywhere together. I don't even remember when that stopped. I thought it was because of the children and lack of available baby sitters that made it change. Then he made friends with Gary and they liked going to sports bars to watch the games together. That's what he said. I was alright with that because I was busy with work and the children.

I wish he had told me that I wasn't enough: slim enough, cute enough, wild enough, or happy enough. I was happily going along with my daily duties. I stopped noticing that he didn't speak when he came in or when he left. He was just preoccupied with his thoughts, I thought. I was surely preoccupied with mine.

I felt like running and screaming up and down the streets of our neighborhood. I wanted to talk to someone but knew there was no one to tell because my best friend had just walked out the door.

I imagined that I could have yelled at him as he walked away. I could have gotten loud and talked crazy. I could have threatened him but none of that was me. I just stood there like a lump on a log- stunned.

I went and soaked in the tub. It would have been a good time to drink some alcohol if I had taken up drinking. But since I didn't drink soaking in the tub had to suffice. I wondered how long it had taken him to work this out. There I was thinking about him when I should have been figuring out my next move. My habit had been to take care of everyone else before thinking of me. I needed to stop. Just stop it, I said to myself. Talking to myself in the tub was not a good look.

I had to start thinking of me. I cried every night for about a month. I prayed that my lonely tears would wash the pain away. Friends came over. Parents helped. Talked to myself but no one could get me out of the slump.

Then I decided to get myself together. I enrolled in night school to get another degree. My parents kept the children. Somehow I made it work.

I got to know myself. I was not just someone's mother or someone's wife or someone's daughter or co-worker. I got to know who I was and what was important to me for me. I was enough.

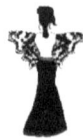

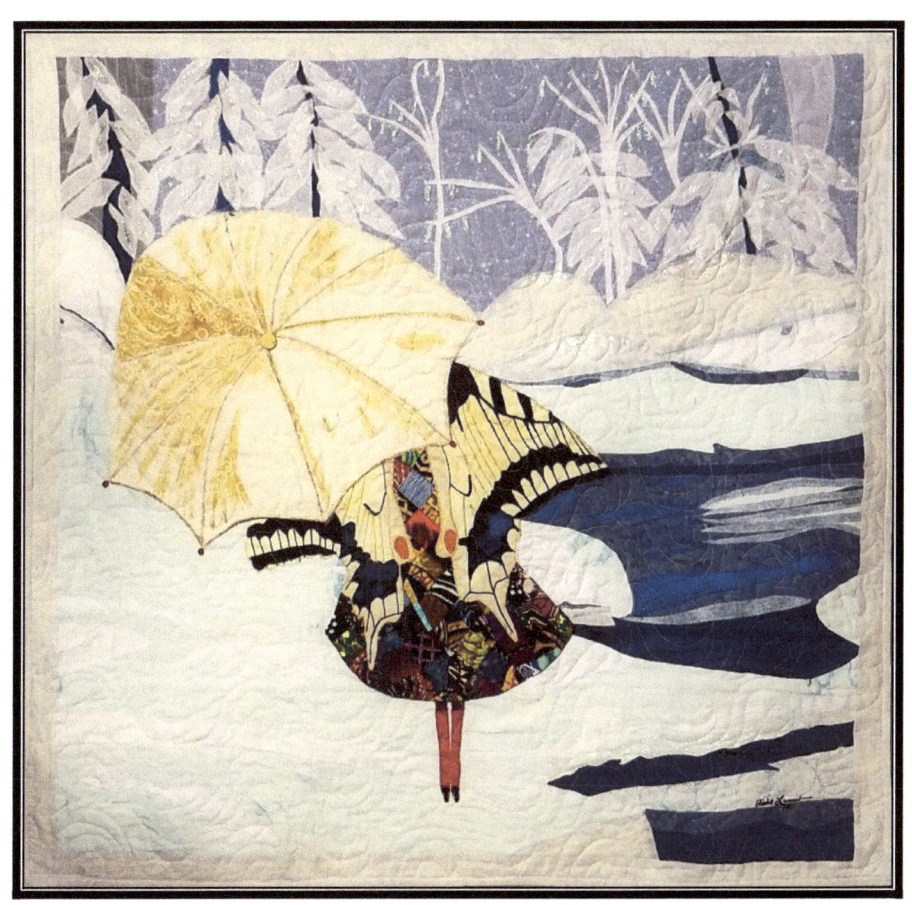

20
WINTER WALK

My mother said I was born in the snow. I am pretty sure she meant that it was a wintry snowy day. She certainly would not have been outside on a snowy bank giving birth to her darling little girl. She didn't even like cold inside the house.

I have loved the snow as far back as I can remember. The day my mother died, I came out and walked in the snow. It was soothing to me. I looked closely at how the ice dripped to the edge of the tree branches and slipped just over the edge.

When I was a little girl, I would run and jump and then roll around in the snow. I loved the clean crisp smell of the air. I wanted to stay out and play all day but my mother would call me in after a while. "You are going to be a frozen ice statue, if I don't watch you," Mother would say.

I could have coined the phrase-Winter Wonderland. The snow has certainly been my friend. Whenever I got bogged down with a thought, I retreated to the snow to take a Winter Walk.

I fell in love very young. They say when you fall you will break something. Well, I fell. I was just out of high school and he was a smooth talking good looking brother that came around the store where I worked every day. "Hi my name is Howard," he said with his hand outstretched. I could have melted. I fell for his dreamy eyes and wonderful promises. My dad always said I was pretty but I was blown away by Howard saying so.

As soon as we were married he whisked me away to Florida. It was a long way from my snow and my family. I knew I would be happy as long as we were together.

Howard changed the moment we moved into our new home. I wanted to make a great impression after we moved into our house. I greeted him with a big smile and what I thought were kind words. "The sound of your voice gets on my nerves," he said. I covered my mouth with my hand and began to keep it shut as much as possible.

Then Howard started to stay out all the time and come home intoxicated. That was when I realized that his fists were quicker than his temper. If I said anything, he'd knock me down. The first time, I couldn't believe that he hit me, but the hitting became more and more frequent. I was afraid and did not know which way to turn.

Mrs. Jackie, the next door neighbor, caught me taking the trash out one day. "Hi neighbor, would you like to come over and share a glass of lemonade" she asked. Sure, I said. I needed to interact with someone. I walked across the grass in our yard to a nicely laid brick walkway in her yard. It lead right up to her kitchen door.

Mrs. Jackie's house was so pleasant. Flowering plants were all around. It felt calm and peaceful. She poured lemonade into two glasses that she pulled from the cabinet and sprinkled a little ice in. Before I drank half the glass, she said that she heard me screaming one night. I dropped my head and didn't respond. "I know it is none of my business," she said politely. "But I just want you to know that I am here to help if you need it." I thanked her for the lemonade and hurried back across the lawn to our house. I still had a little pride at that point.

The late nights had turned into entire weekends away. When Howard returned on Monday he would be cold and mean. Mondays were my weekly nightmares. I could do nothing right, but the end of my patience was near. I hadn't realized it consciously but something inside of me was different.

Howard raised his hand and I fought back. Something inside me had clicked. It was the worst beating of all. I was bleeding and hurt. I sat in the corner of the bedroom and didn't dare move. He seemed to have some kind of pain inside him that drove him crazy. I called it "Passed-Down Pain". Only this time one of the neighbors called the Police. I bet I know which one.

The doorbell rang and he answered promptly. Two policemen said they had been called about a disturbance at this house. He turned on the charm and said, " you know how women can get sometimes. We just had a little disagreement." One of the policeman said, " I know what you mean. My wife acts up sometimes too." The other one said, "we have to take a look around. It's routine."

"Okay," Howard responded. Second policeman walked into the room where I was hunched in a corner. First policeman asked what he found. He said, "just a woman." They laughed and left.

Friday took so long to come, but as soon as it did, I was knocking on Mrs. Jackie's door. I told her that I wanted to go back home to my family. She was more than glad to help. She bought me a plane ticket and took me to the airport the very next day. Howard came home to an empty house on Monday.

Home was good. The first snow welcomed me. I couldn't wait to take a long walk. The crunch of snow under my feet was music to my ears. I went over to one of the trees and thumped the snowy branches. I delighted in the mist. I slipped off my gloves and felt the icy cold in my palms.

Mounds of snow piled up everywhere made me feel so safe. I felt like running and jumping and rolling in the snow but I was too old to do that.

I thought I needed a man to complete me. I found out that I was complete within myself and another person can add to my journey but not make me whole.

I am happy with me.

21
PATTERN
STANDING TALL

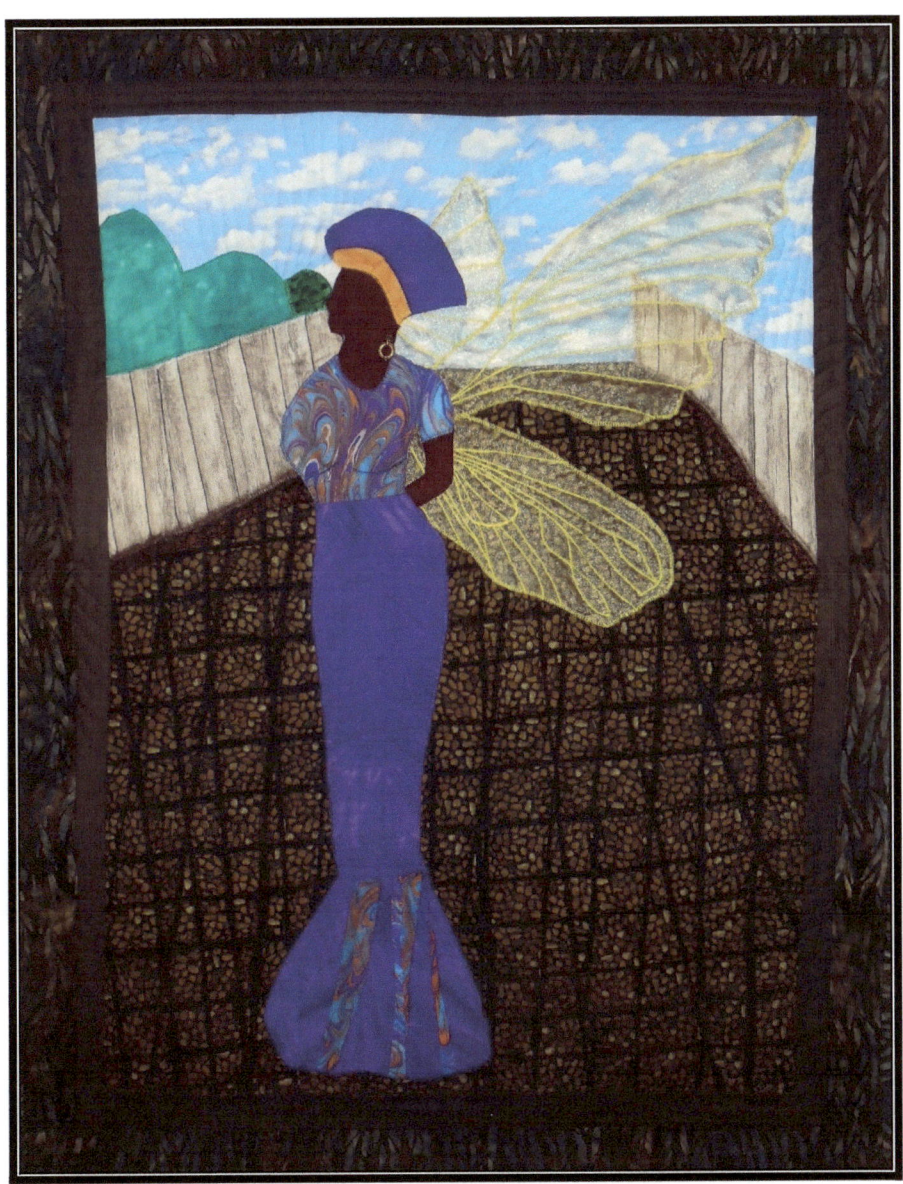

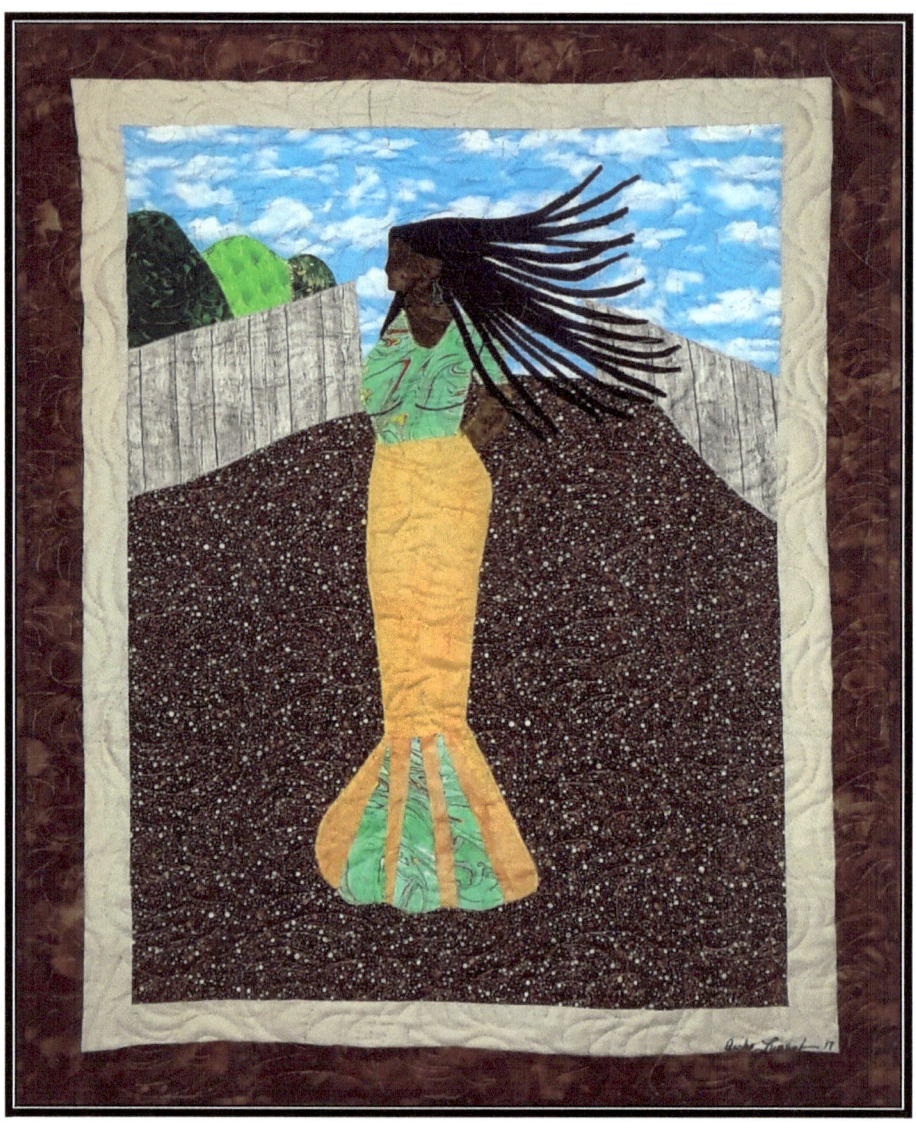

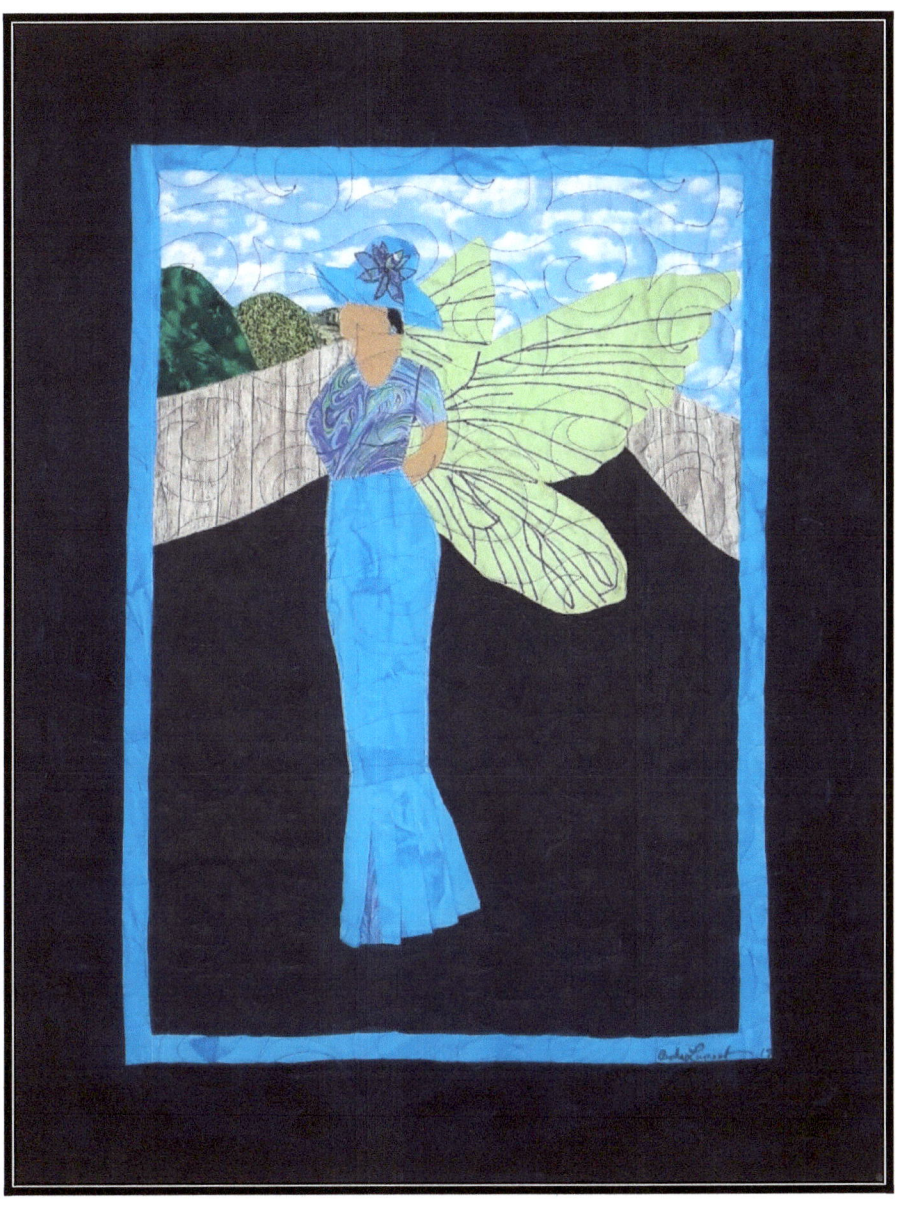

Approximate Size 30" x 36-38"

Fabric needed

Sky	¼ yard blue sky
Ground	¾ yard your choice
Fence	½ yard brown
Blouse and trim	1-2 Itty Bitties* or 1/8 yard
Skirt and hat	¼ yard
Hat (optional)	1/8 yard color your choice
Hair (instead of hat)	1/8 yard black or brown
Wings (optional)	½ yard sheer or cotton
Face and arms	1/8 yard brown
Trees/greenery	1/8 yard green-equivalent scraps

*Itty Bitties are marbled fabric created by Marquetta Johnson of Atika Arts.

1. Copy or print pages 102 through 114. Pattern numbers 12, 13 and 16 are blank. Use blank sheet of paper to fill in space.

2. Tape all pages together using black border lines as guide to make a complete picture pattern.

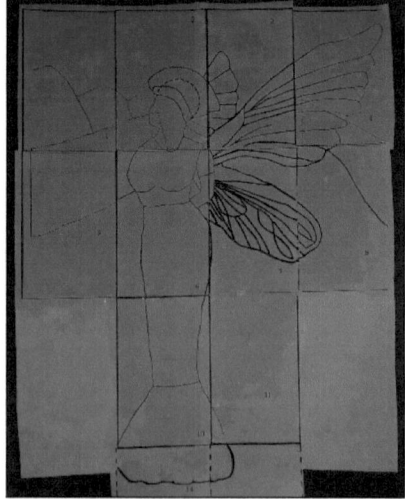

3. Draw or trace each pattern piece (hat, blouse, skirt, wings, fence, head and arm patterns) from the complete picture. Overlapping pieces are shown with dotted lines. Add ¼" seam allowance where applicable. I dotted allowances needed.

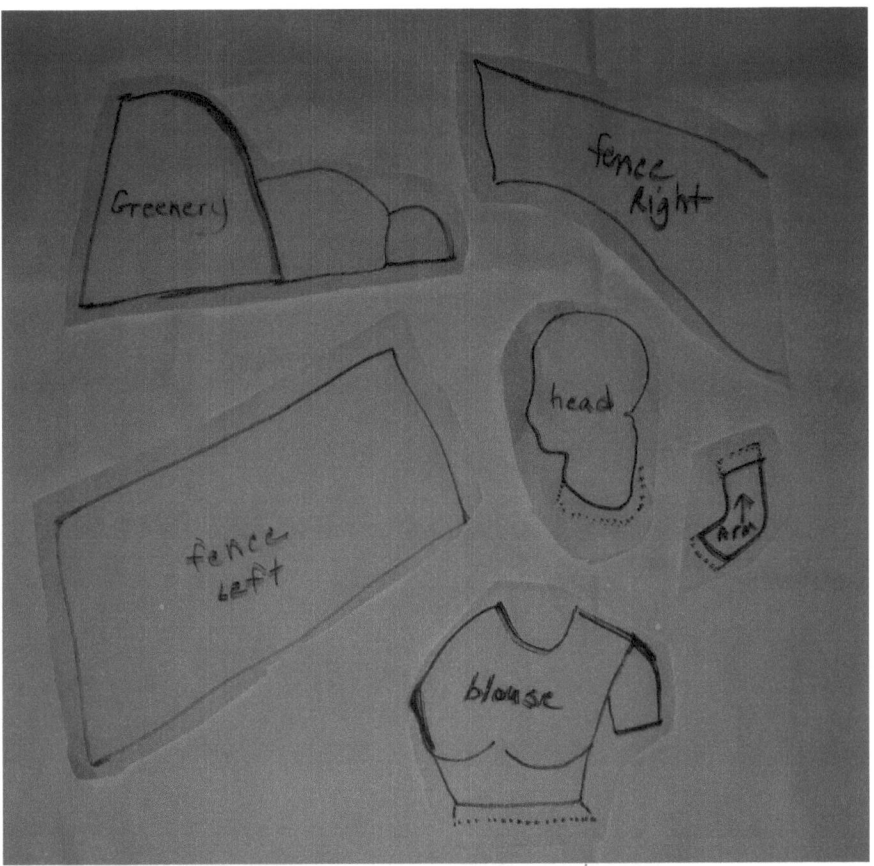

Note: Not actual size needed for pattern.

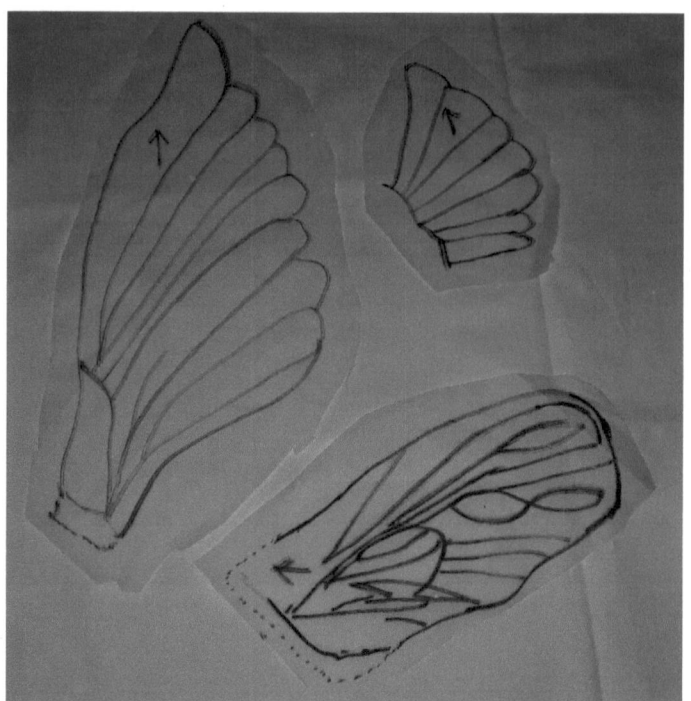

Note: Not actual size needed for pattern.

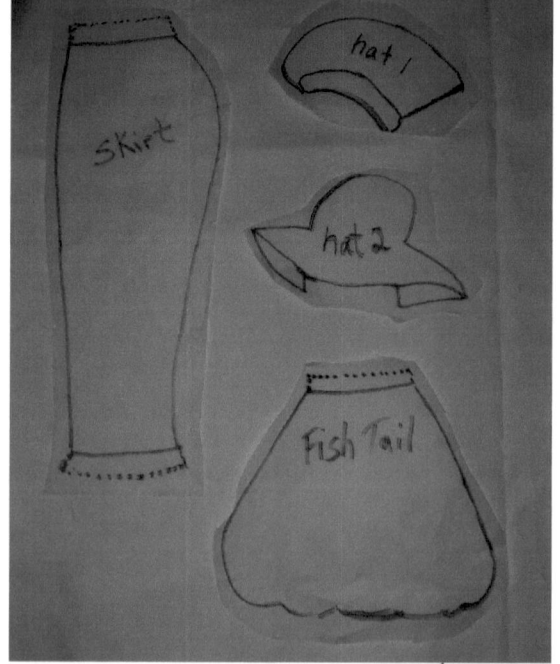

Be creative and draw lines for slits in fish tail.

4. Cut sky fabric 21" x 9". Cut ground fabric 21" X 24"
Make background first by attaching ground fabric to

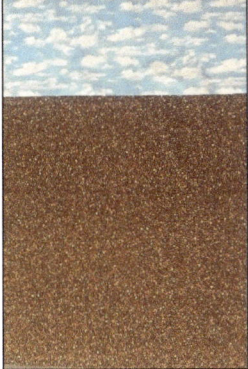

sky fabric.

5. Put fence in place over background pieces as shown below. Place greenery and slip bottom edge under top of fence. Top stitch fence pieces in place. Then stitch greenery in place. I use different colors of green but you can make it all one piece.

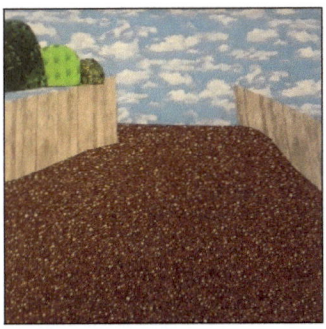

6. Place wings if used. Stitch in place. I pin the head in place to keep with where other pieces go. If you use a sheer fabric the wings will seem transparent.

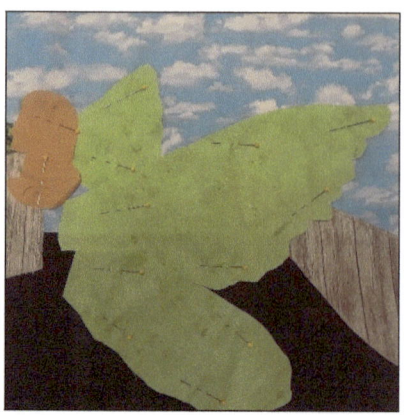

I use Gift Wrapping Tissue Paper to trace wings and show veins. Use a single stitch thread to show the veins. Peel paper away.

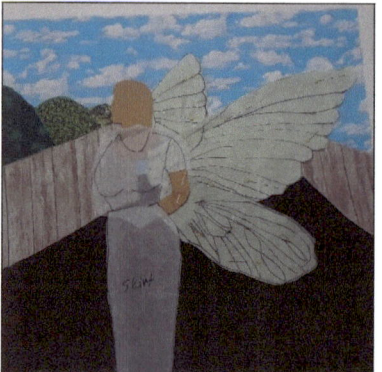 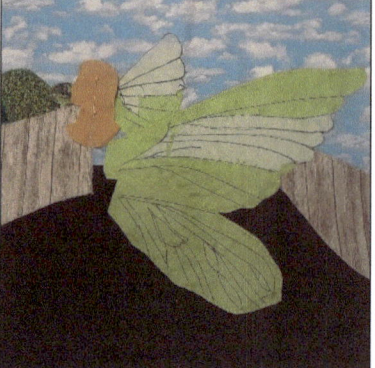

7. Then satin stitch or zig zag the veins using a different color thread.

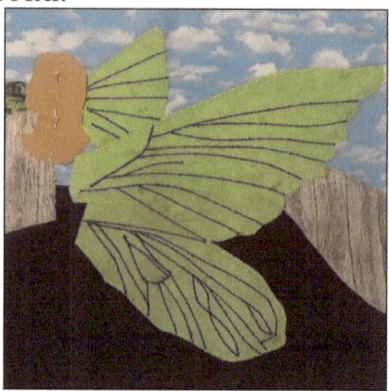

8. No Wings. Move head over a little to center when hair is included. Sew head on tucking the neck under blouse.

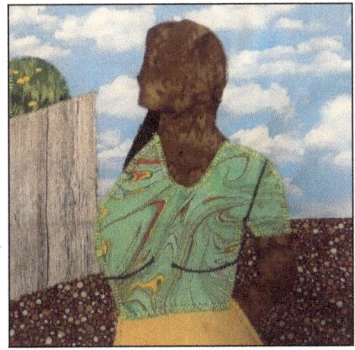

9. Make skirt with either fish tail or pleated tail.
Instructions for fish tail
Cut from pattern adding ¼" seam allowance to each piece. Sew pieces together. Add to skirt.

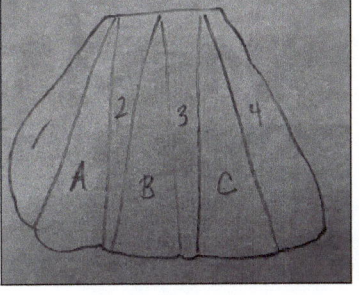
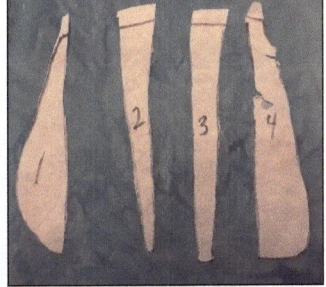

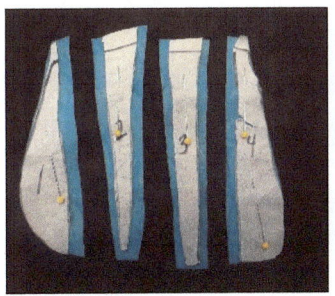
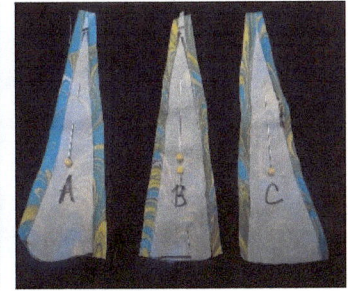

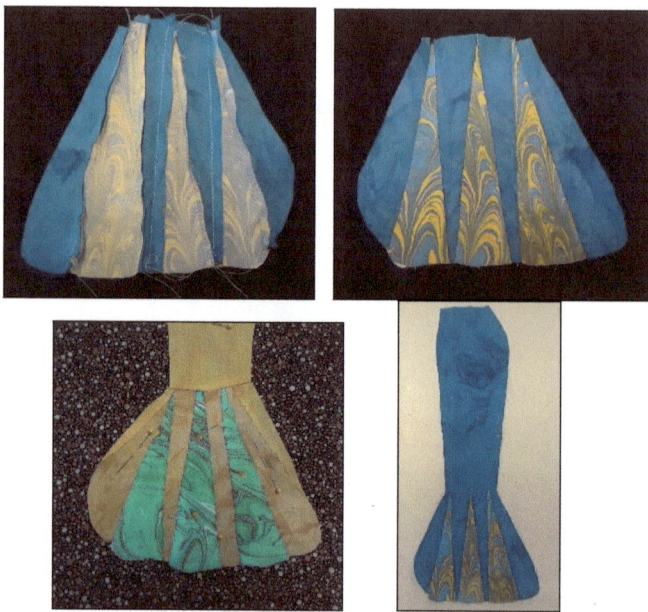

Instructions for pleated tail

Cut one 12" x 6 ½" piece same as the skirt. Cut it in five 2 ½ pieces. Then cut four 1 ½" x 6 ½" strips of fabric same as blouse. Sew pieces together. Fold on the seams to create pleats. Add to skirt.

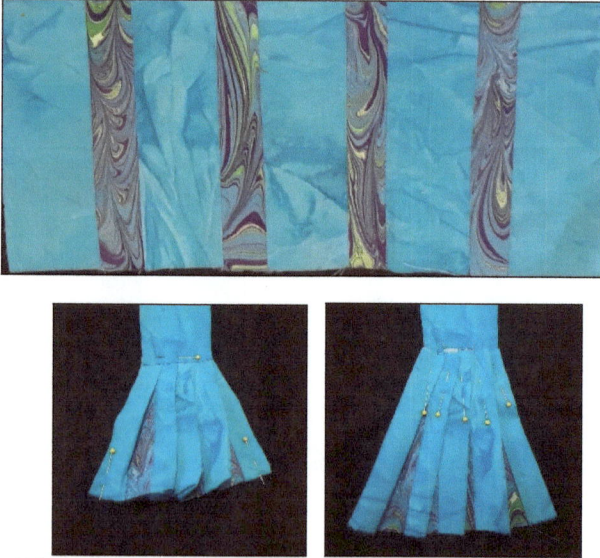

I hem by hand but can be machine stitched

10. Stick neck inside blouse before pinning. Pin blouse to skirt and arm to background. Straight stitch with paper first. Remove paper and zig zag highlights.

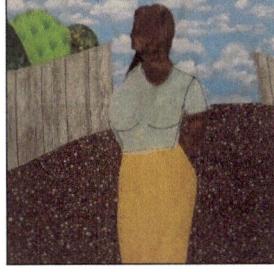

11. Make hair or hat. Add hair one strand at a time. Add small amount of fabric for hair under hat 2. Sew to the head.

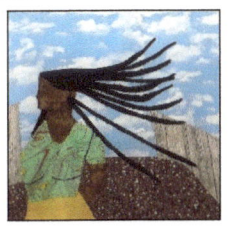 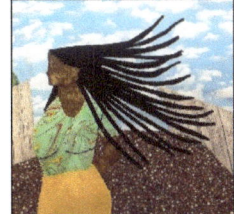 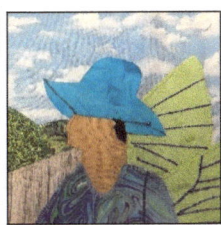

12. Add first border on the quilt. Cut it between 1½" to 2½" (your choice of size). I like two borders but you have the option to use only one.

13. Add second border on the first border. Cut between 2" to 4" (your choice of size).

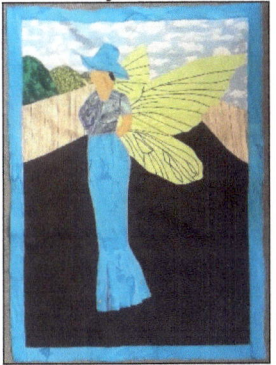 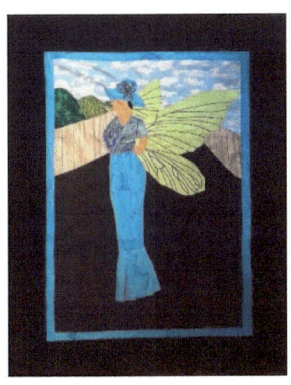

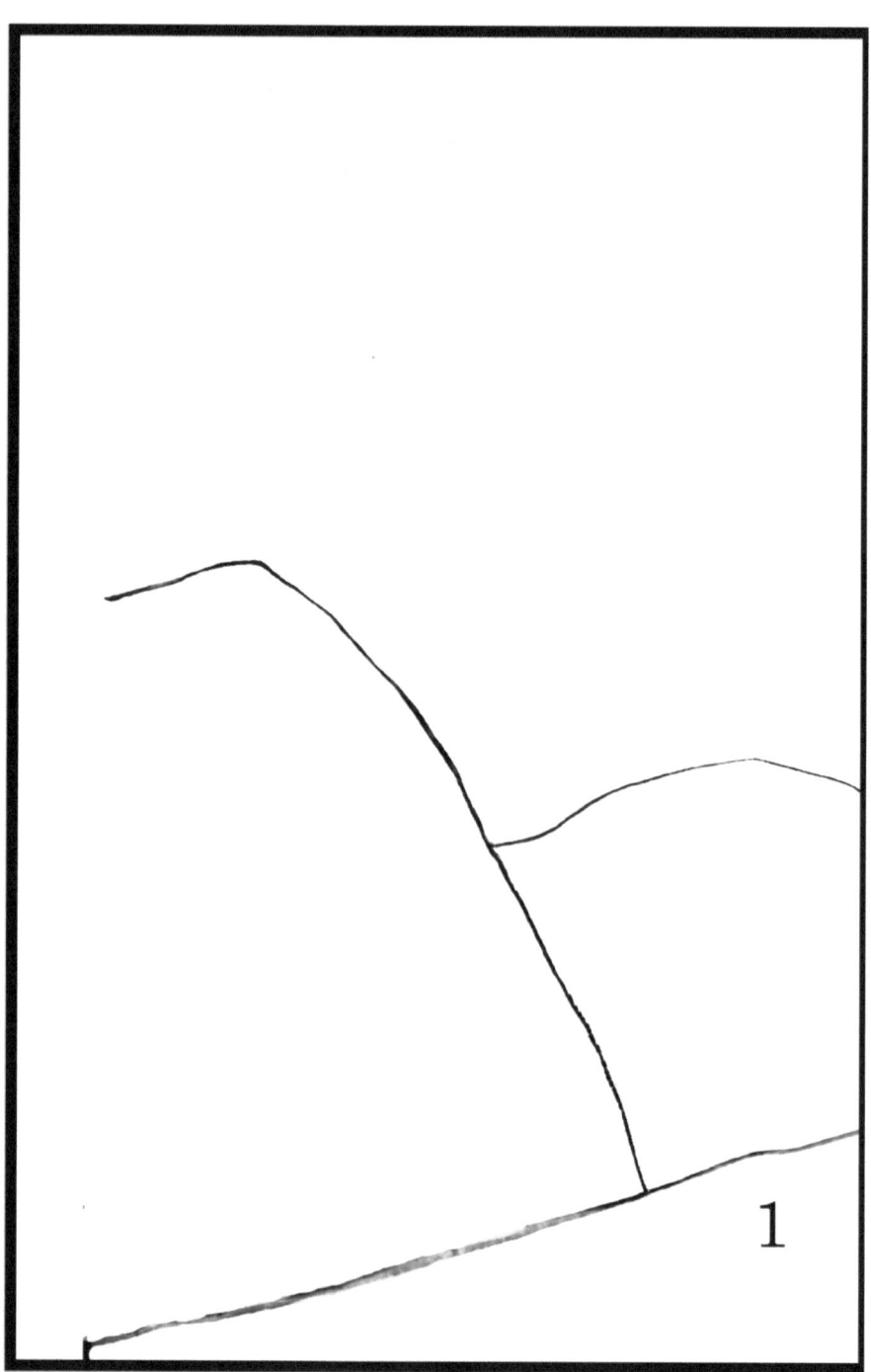

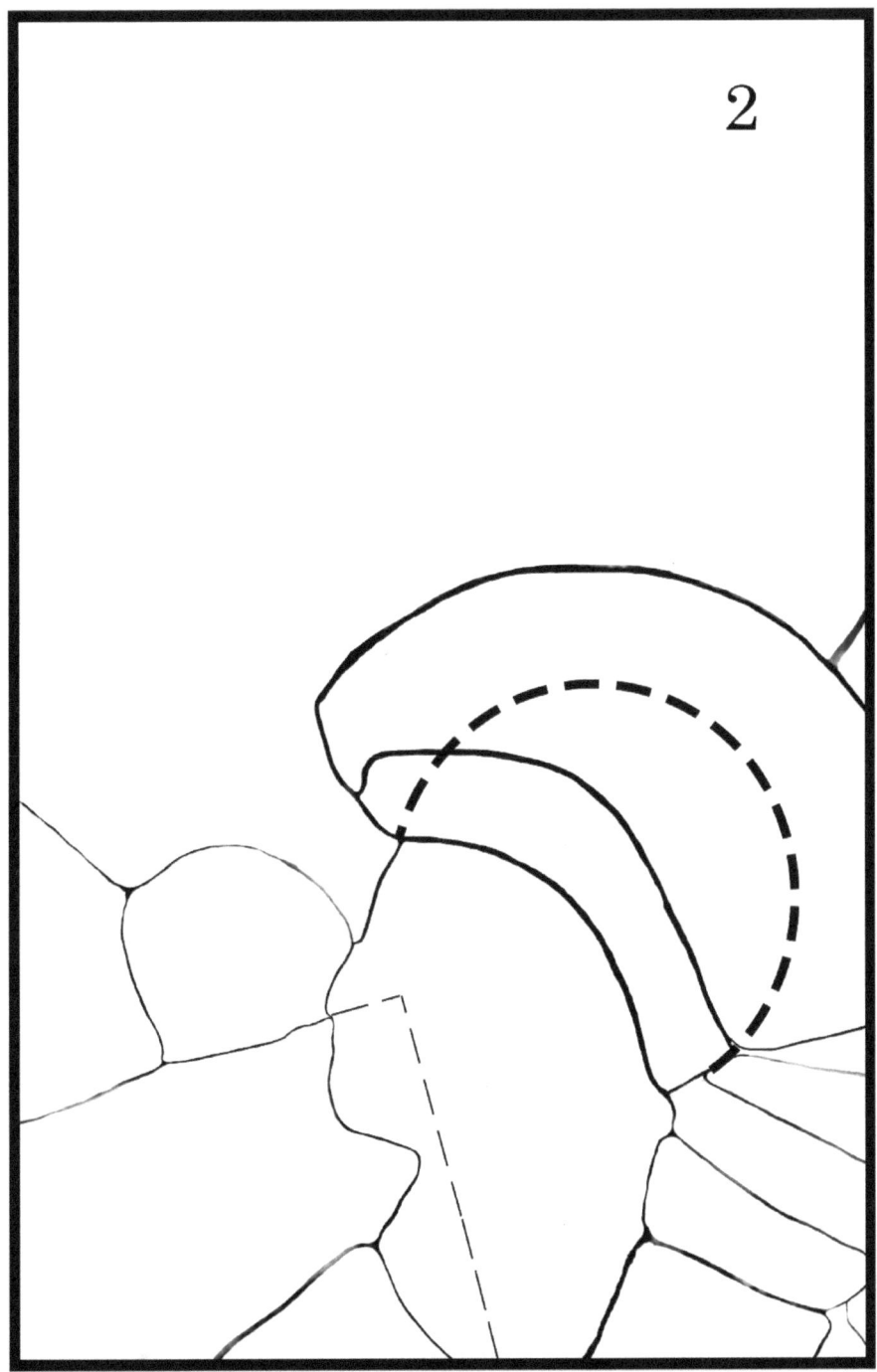

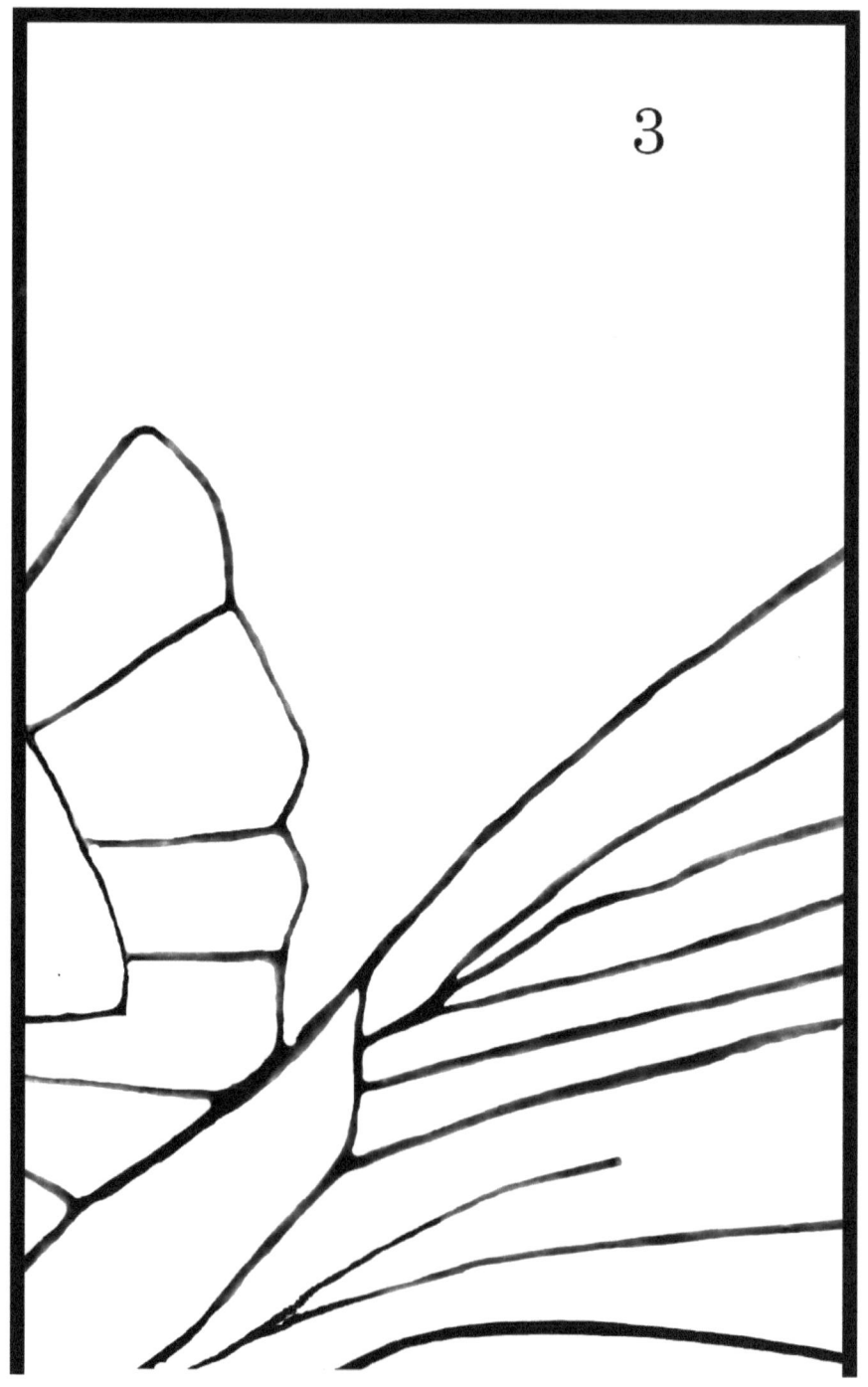

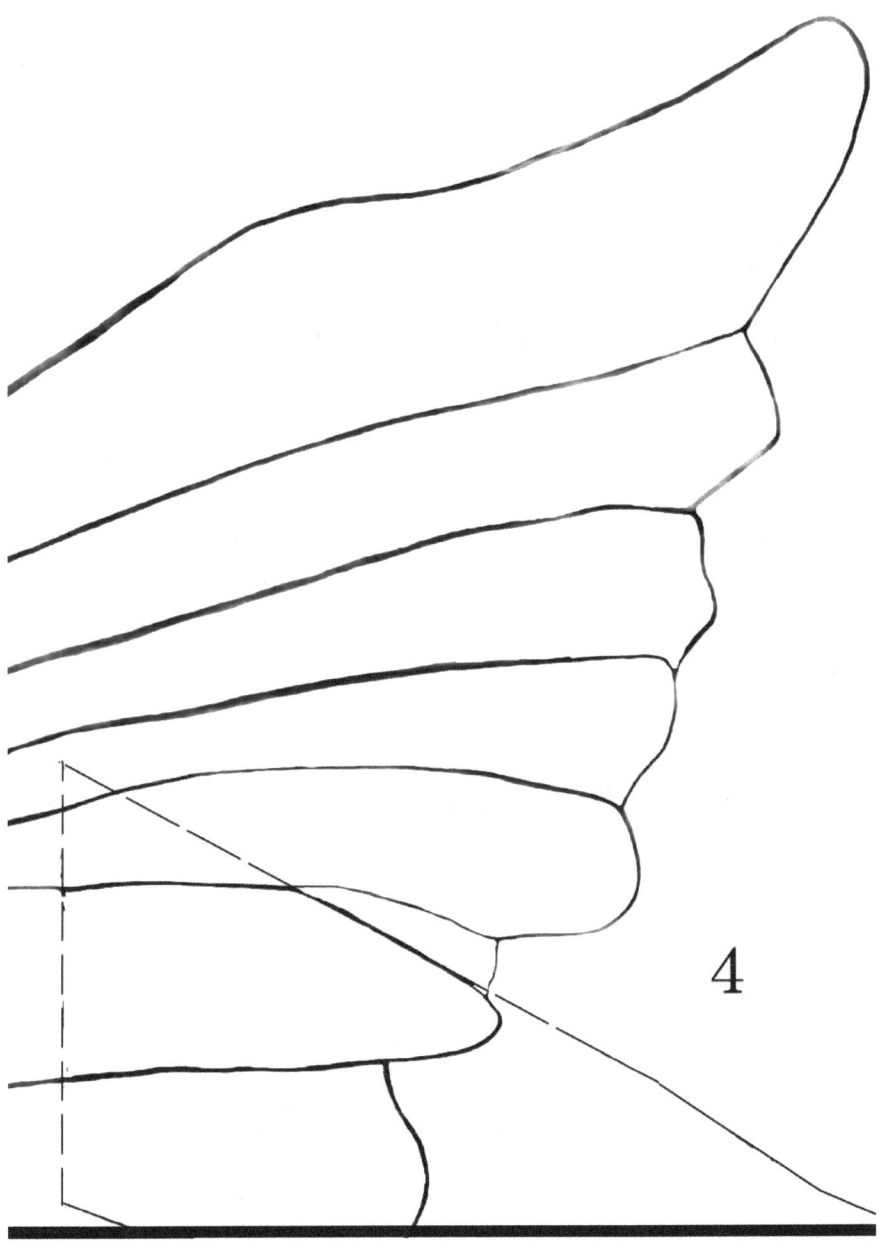

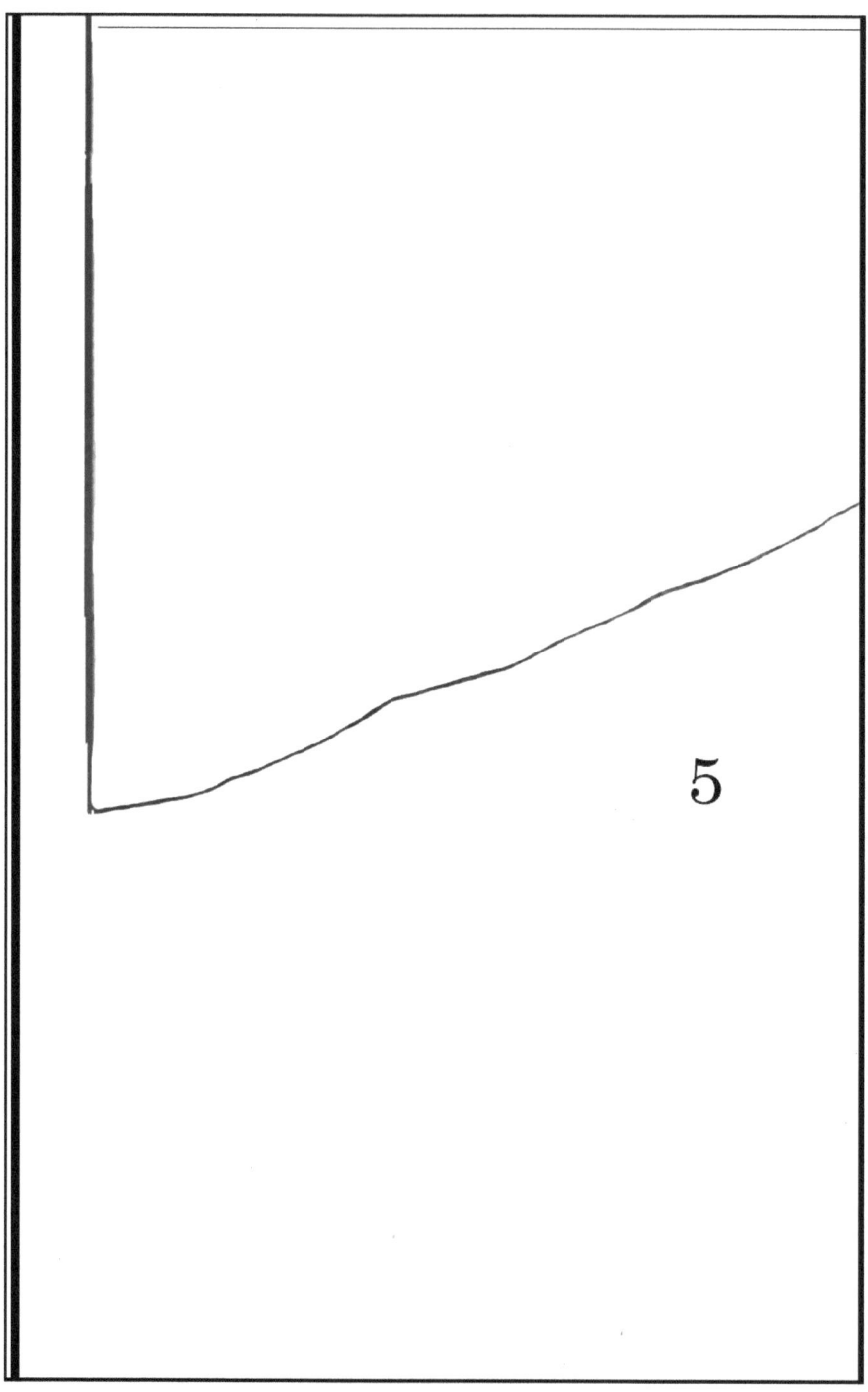

5

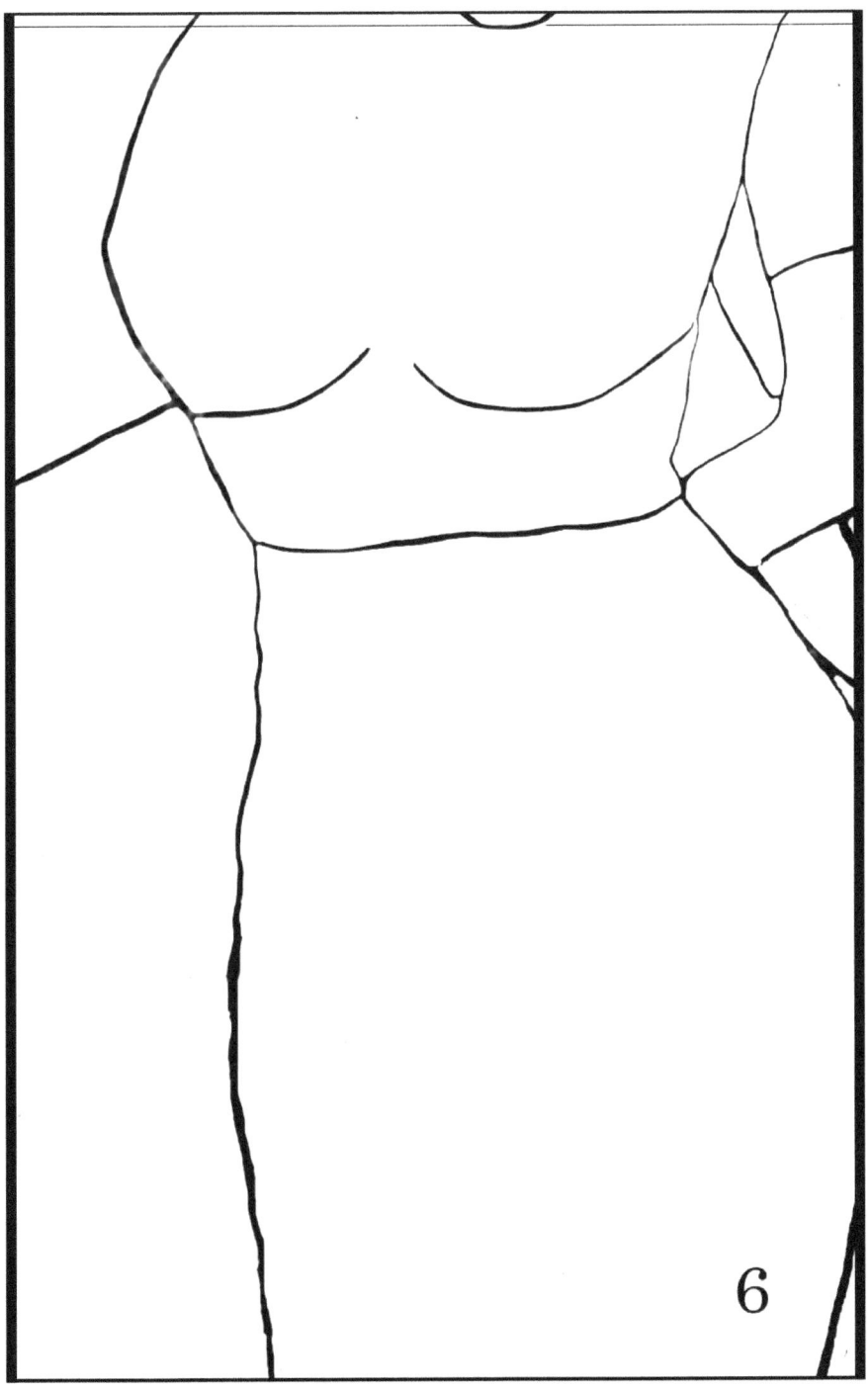

6

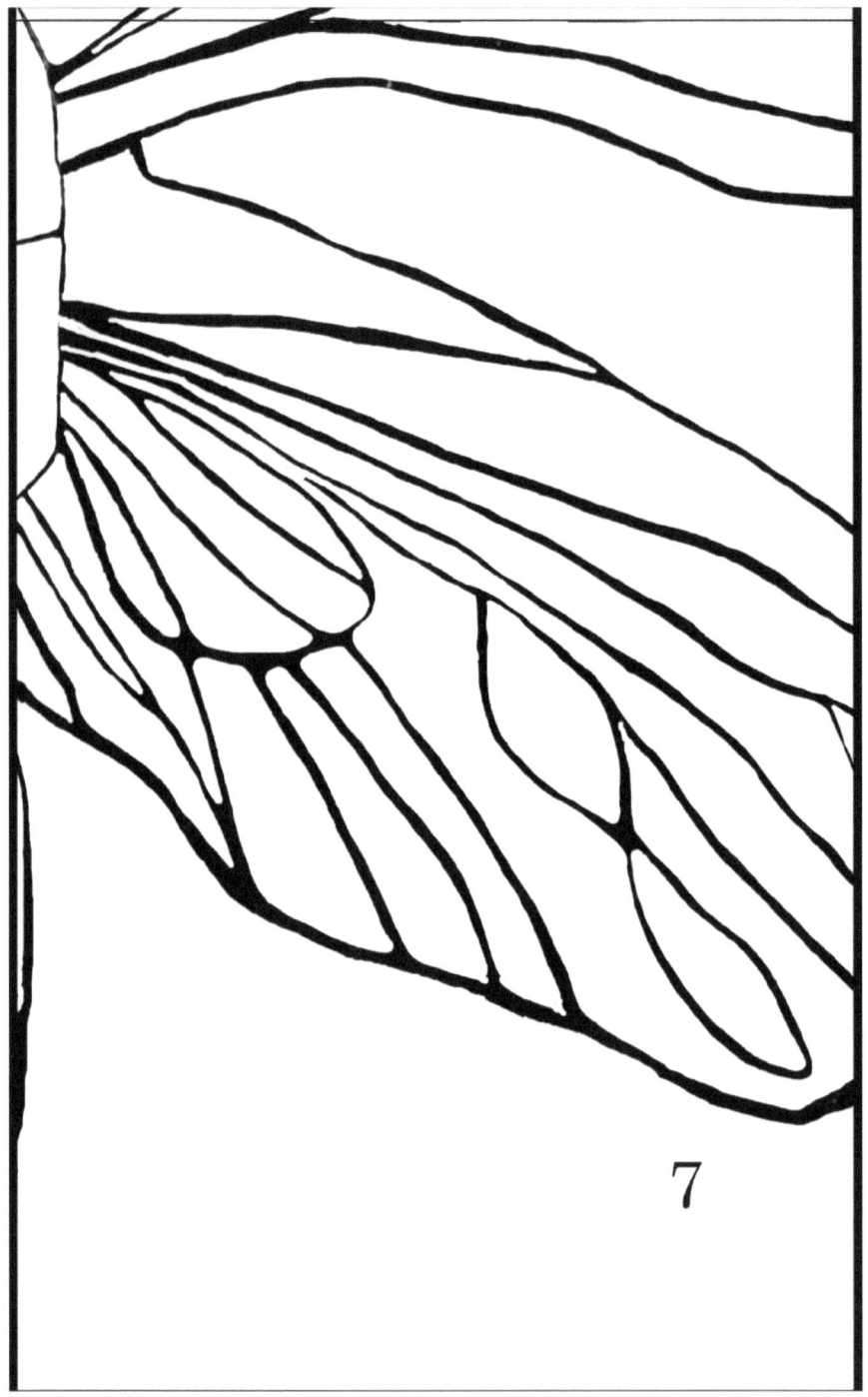

7

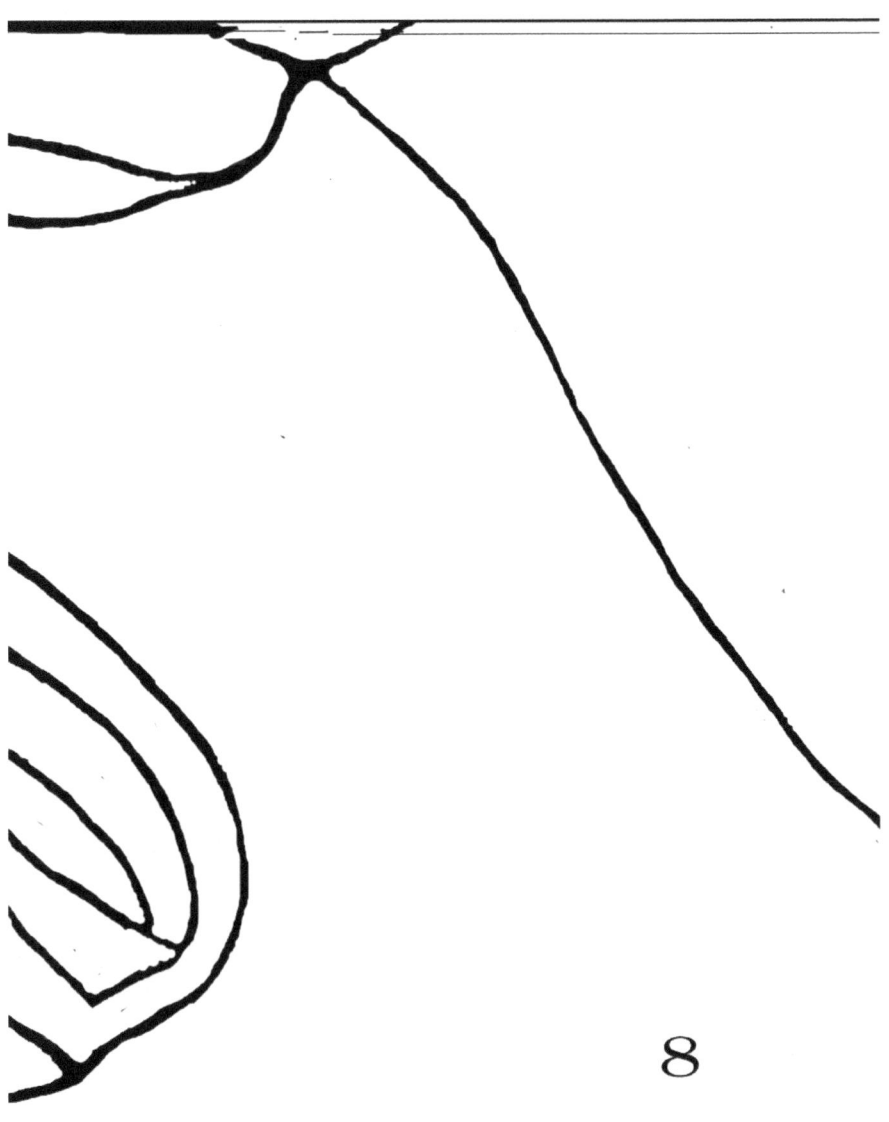

8

9

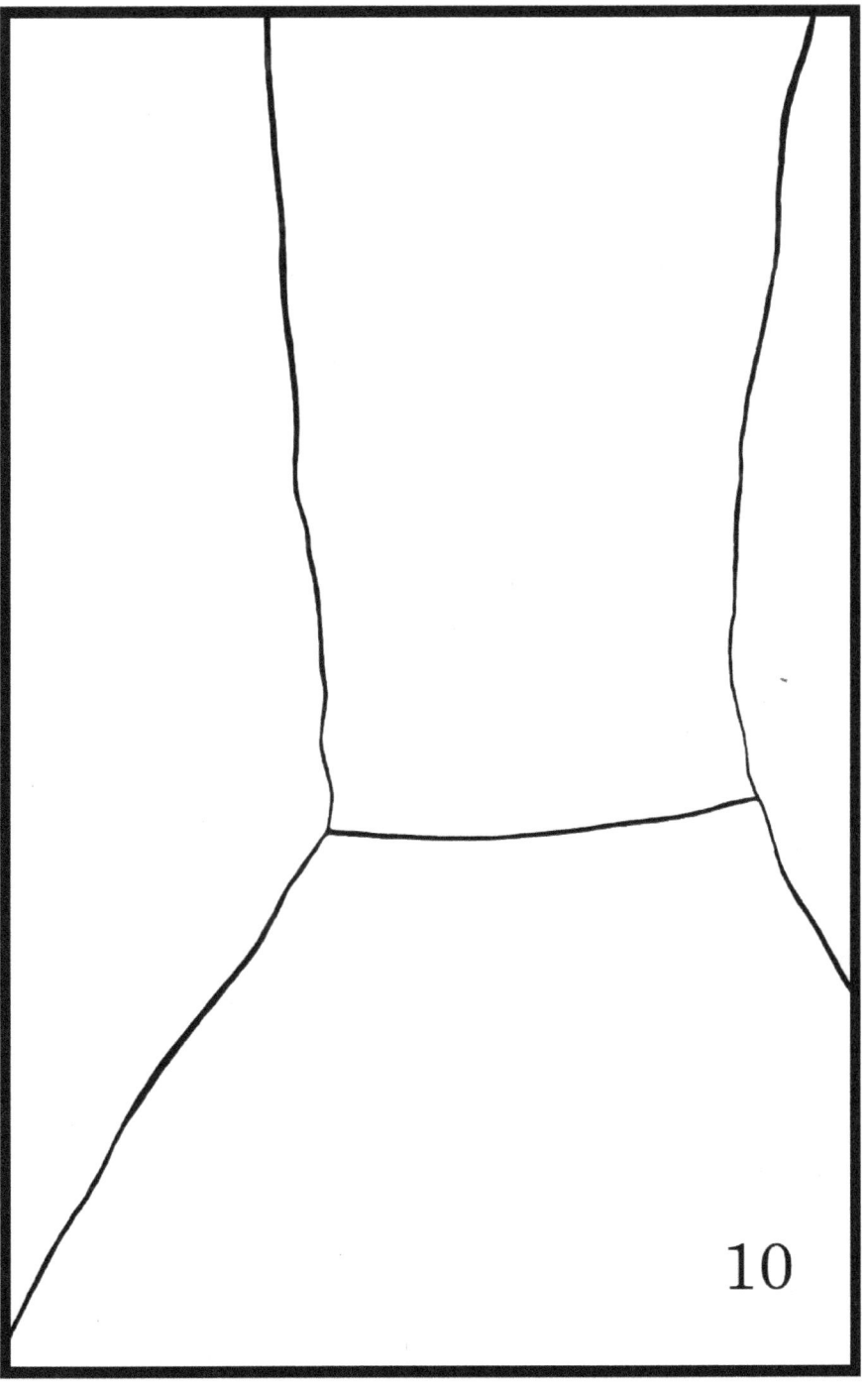

10

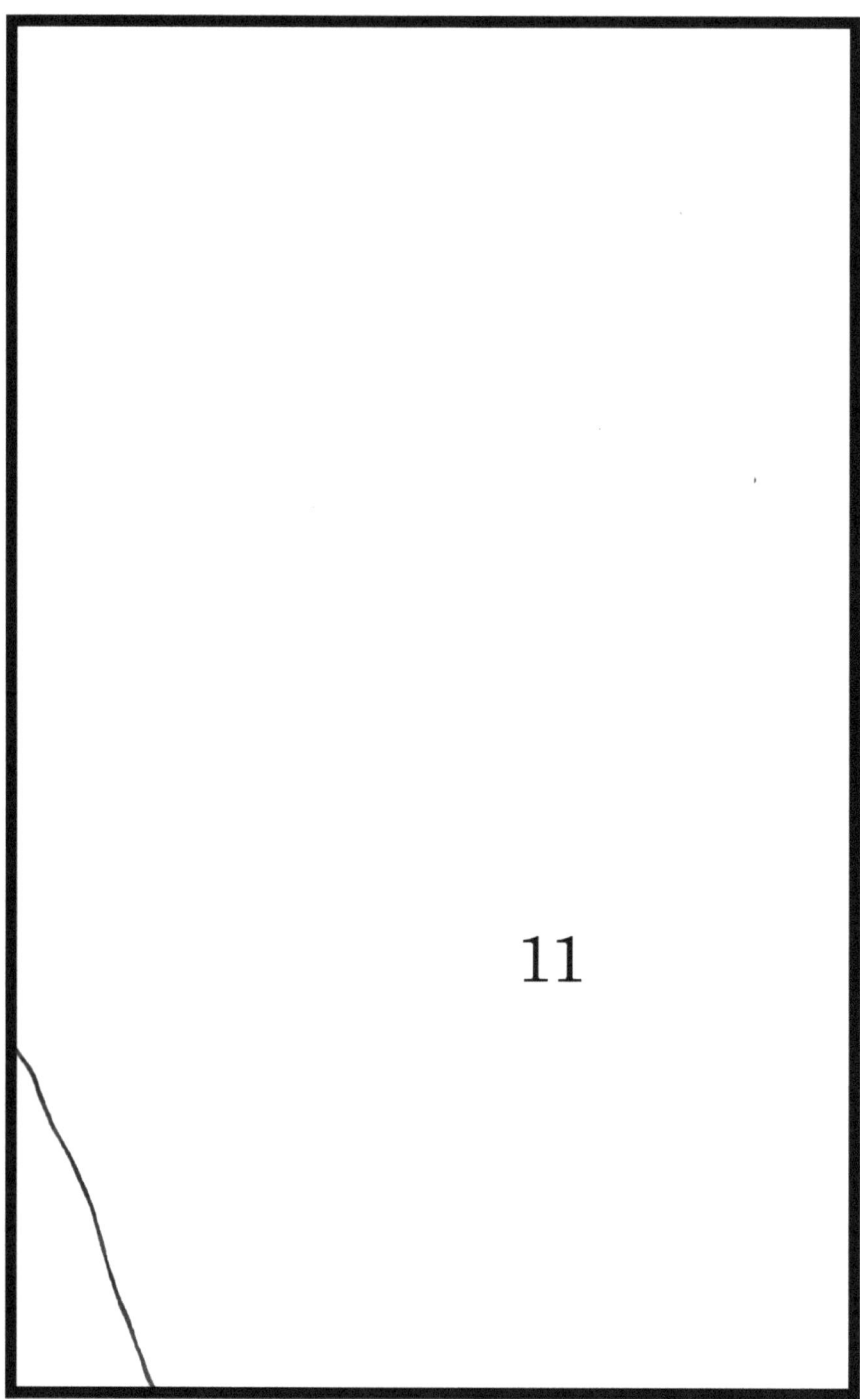

11

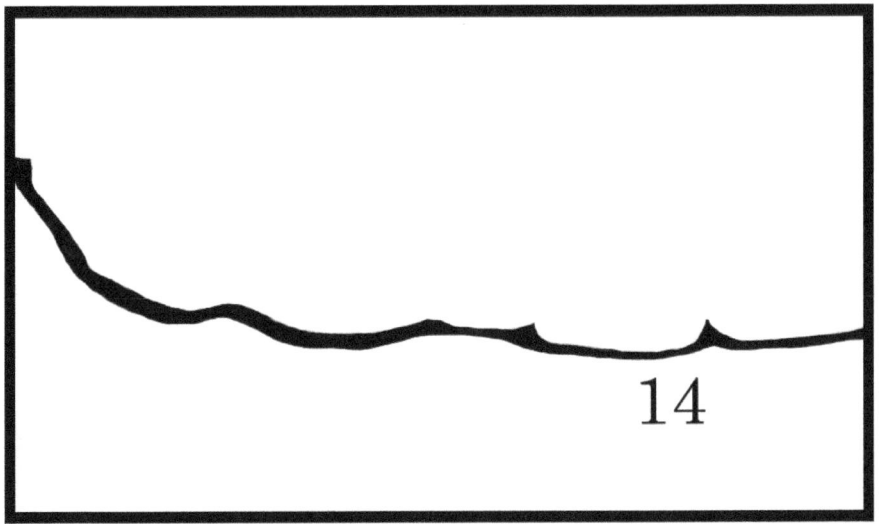

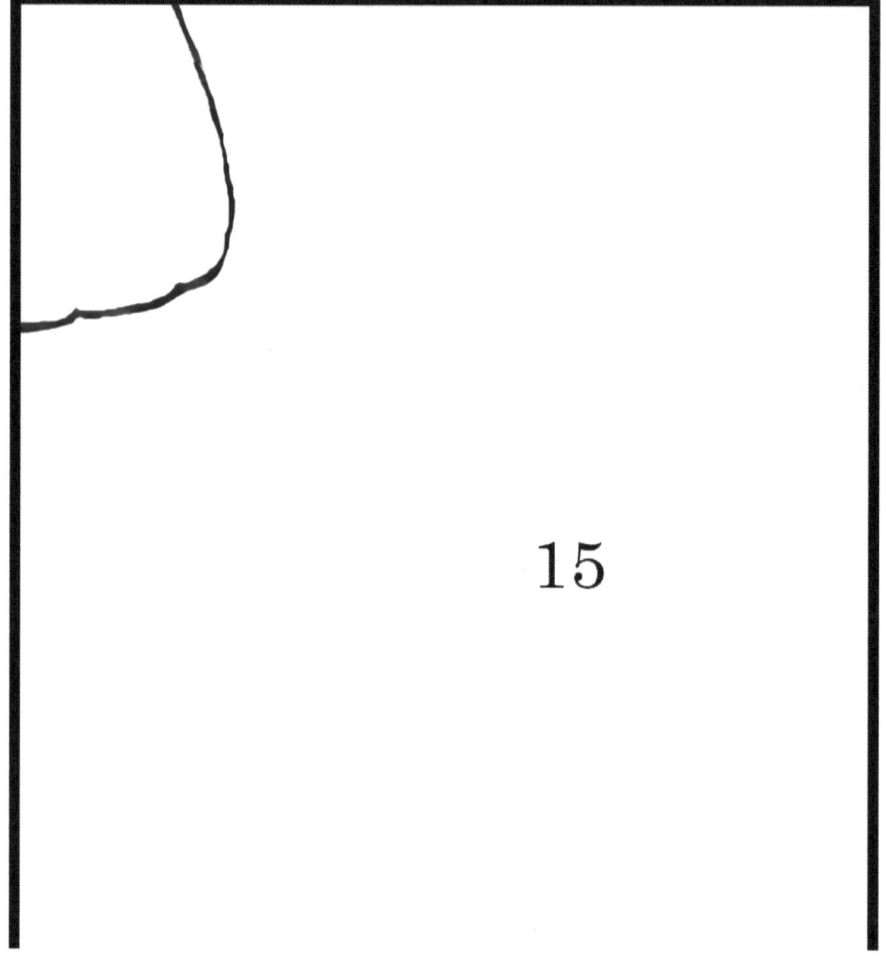

15

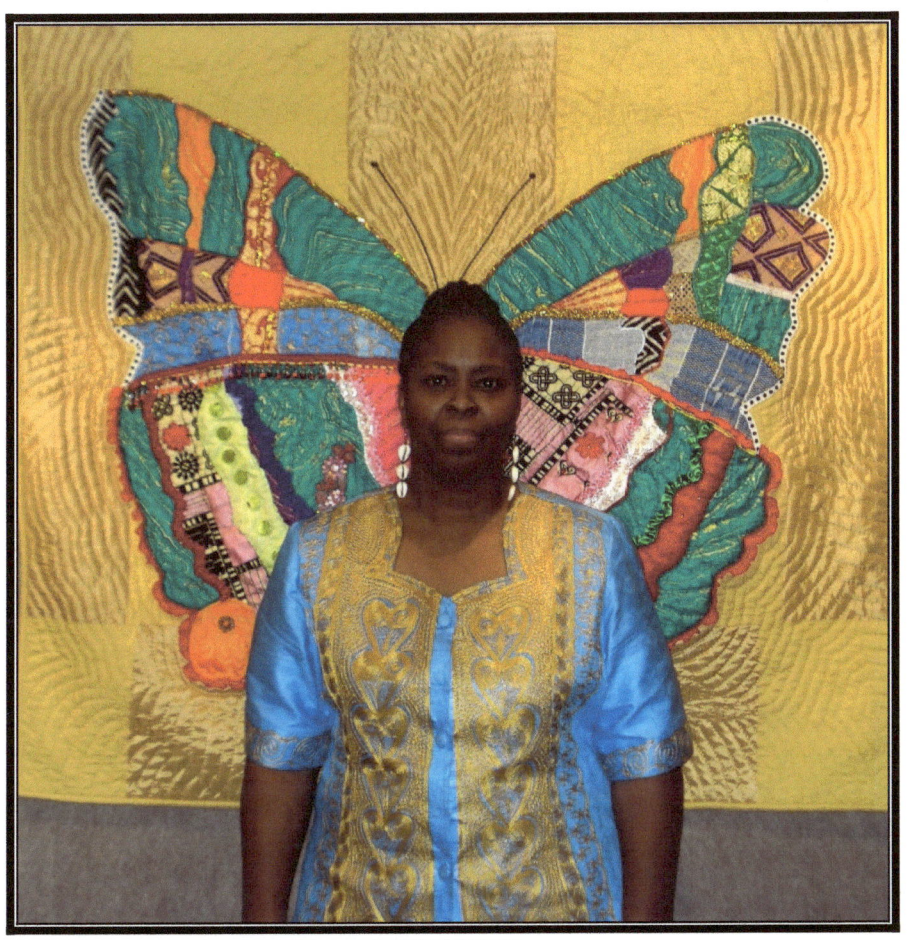

AUTHOR

Aisha Lumumba is a well-known artist residing in
Atlanta, Georgia USA. She was born in a rural suburb of
Atlanta, known as McDonough. She loves writing and
quilting, which led her to write stories and books about
quilting. Ms. Lumumba started writing in Elementary
School and continues to the present day. She has more
than 40 years of quilting experience, not only for practical
uses, but as a form of artistic expression.

Ms. Lumumba is very prolific as a quilter and fiber artist. She is a member of the Brown Sugar Stitchers Quilt Guild. Her quilts are now a part of the collections of Ambassador Andrew Young, Mrs. Valerie Jackson, Dr. Stephanie Jolly, Dr. Jualene Dodson, Ms. Brenda Banks, Ms. Woodie Persons, The Atrium on Sweet Auburn, President & Mrs. Barack Obama and many others.

Other books by Aisha Lumumba

Afterwhile: The Secrets of a Women's Heart,

Cuisine on the Nile Vegetarian Cookbook,

Gifted: Art Quilts featuring African American History Makers

If Quilts Could Talk: My Quilts, My Stories Volume 1

Scrap Easy: Building A Collage Quilt

Inspired By Her: Celebrating Femininity through Art Quilts